ALOHA
KITCHEN

ALOHA
KITCHEN

Recipes from Hawai'i

ALANA KYSAR

PHOTOGRAPHS BY ALANA KYSAR AND BROOKLYN DOMBROSKI

TEN SPEED PRESS
California | New York

CONTENTS

To my mom, my dad, Moses, and Vienna Sausage—you guys are my everything.
And to anyone who loves Hawai'i—this book is for you.

ALOHA

Aloha [ə ˈlo.hə]: hello! E komo mai (welcome to) *Aloha Kitchen*.

This Hawaiian word *aloha* means so much. It means love and affection, kindness and compassion, mercy and sympathy, pity and grace, and is also used as a greeting or farewell. It's a feeling, a state of mind, an attitude, and a way of life. It's even Hawai'i's official nickname—the Aloha State! The aloha spirit, as defined by a state statute, "is the coordination of mind and heart within each person. It brings each person to the self. Each person must think and emote good feelings to others." Aloha must be extended with no obligation in return, and to live aloha, you must "hear what is not said, see what cannot be seen, and know the unknowable." This guiding principle of friendliness and acceptance of ideas and cultures extends to all aspects of life in the islands, from friendships to family and even to the kitchen. This way of life—placing the aloha spirit at the core of relationships and actions—is what truly makes Hawai'i a special place. This spirit is the core of these recipes and this book.

When I set out to write this book, I wanted to capture the spirit of aloha through practice. So I opened up our kitchen and home to friends (new and old), family, and really anyone who wanted to come. We hosted no-frills, paper-napkin dinners almost weekly. Our friends and family tried most of the foods in this book during various stages of development. Sometimes the recipes didn't exactly work out; other times they were much better. But no matter the case, we got together and made a great night out of it. There is a very long island between my kitchen and the dining room, and I am thankful to each and every friend who sat on the kitchen stools, chatting, while I toiled away at the recipes. Many parties, throughout the yearlong process of writing this book, were graced with aloha kitchen treats. At the end of the process, *Aloha Kitchen* felt like the only title worthy of this book and our shared experiences represent the spirit of Hawai'i and why this tiny archipelago has captivated the world.

When you close your eyes and think about Hawai'i, what comes to mind? Do you see the brilliant sapphire and turquoise ocean glistening in the sun? Maybe you think about the feeling of the warm, soft sand between your toes? Do you hear gently rustling palms? Or is your perfect moment when you feel the cool, breezy trade winds collide with the warm, light blanket of humidity that hugs the Hawaiian Islands chain? Even if you've never been to Hawai'i, you have an idea of how these iconic islands— Hawai'i (the Big Island), Maui, Moloka'i, Lāna'i, Kaho'olawe O'ahu, Kaua'i, and Ni'ihau—look, smell, and feel.

For me, it's the way the islands taste. The first thing that comes to mind is my mother's mochiko chicken, triangle musubi (onigiri), and potato mac salad. A close second might be a Spam musubi, but let's talk about that later. My Hawai'i is the smoky and sweet smell of a pig roasting in an imu, a traditional outdoor underground oven. That distinctive aroma is built upon layers of kiawe wood, sopping wet banana stumps, hot lava rocks, and, of course, all the delicious meats cooking oh-so-slowly. I haven't lived on the islands in recent years, but I can still recall who makes the best pork and peas or chow fun, and I know where I was when I tried my first malasada. That's my Hawai'i, the Hawai'i I remember best.

I enjoyed many of these beloved foods as a sun-kissed, salty-skinned, and barefoot child growing up in Hawai'i. I can trace my earliest years through the many constellations of freckles that paint their way across my face. I was an eighties baby who grew up on the island of Maui, part of one of the most isolated island chains on Earth. I spent my days running around the Kamaole Beach Park in my fluorescent, ruffled two-piece, tip-toeing my way into the bluer-than-blue ocean, breaking past that foamy white shore break with my boogie board. I dedicated hours hunting for crabs in the sugary white sand, and countless more collecting white beach naupaka (half-flower) berries as ammunition for my beach-berry wars. Pretty sure the latter was my equivalent of snowball fights; those little berries stung just as much as their colder-climate cousins.

When I was seven years old, I chased a soccer ball up and down a field and rollerbladed around my parents' garage, dreaming of becoming the next Kristi Yamaguchi. I also had weekly hula lessons where I learned oli (Hawaiian chants) and the dances that helped tell their stories from my kumu hula (teacher). I was ten years old when I learned to play the 'ukulele behind my back, which felt like the absolute coolest thing in the world at the time and still kinda does. When I was thirteen years old, I lost track of how many lei-making-induced finger pricks I'd collected, because those lei for my hula hālau (group's) weekly performances didn't make themselves.

"When you close your eyes and think about Hawai'i, what comes to mind? . . . For me, it's the way the islands taste. The first thing that comes to mind is my mother's mochiko chicken, triangle musubi (onigiri), and potato mac salad."

All these Hawaiian traditions (hula, 'ukulele, lei making) probably have you saying, "Oh, wow! You're Hawaiian!" Well, no—it's a bit more complicated than that. My mother is sansei, or third-generation Japanese American. She was born and raised in Hilo, Hawai'i. And my father is northwestern European, born and raised in Los Angeles, California. That makes me hapa haole, which loosely translates to half white and has come to mean a person of mixed ethnic heritage. While I'm from Hawai'i, I don't have any Hawaiian ancestors and am therefore not considered Hawaiian. I understand that's a bit confusing, since my dad, for instance, is a Californian because he was born and raised in California. However, in Hawai'i, people identify ethnically rather than geographically. Only people who are ethnically Hawaiian are considered Hawaiian. We'll get into the ethnic breakdown of Hawai'i and the origins of various groups later, but for now, I hope that you're still with me.

Because of this geographic identity, the idea that I'm writing a cookbook encompassing the history and cultures of my favorite place in the world is honestly something that terrifies me. It's hard enough to represent yourself, never mind your entire state, and for this reason, I did not embark on this journey lightly. I'm a home cook. I grew up in Kula on the island of Maui with parents who both love to cook. French, Pacific Rim fusion, and local Hawai'i flavors were abundant. With their influence, I learned to love a diverse range of cuisines and, at a young age, spent time helping them prepare dishes. I started with salads (which my father playfully scored for presentation, creativity, and flavor) but quickly graduated to building pommes Anna and roasting chicken. I remember how my mom kept all of our family recipes in a giant folder, and I loved pulling all the pages out and doodling on them, usually in pen.

I was a typical teenager who was desperate to go to college across the all-expansive Pacific Ocean, so my love and appreciation for all things Hawai'i didn't really come until after I had moved away and no longer had access to my mother's amazing mochiko chicken, teriyaki beef sticks, and beef stew. I remember moving out of the dorms for my sophomore year at the University of San Diego and being shocked that many of my friends didn't cook. Most of my friends in college were also from Hawai'i—funnily enough, all of us who couldn't wait to leave home behind ended up hanging out with one another on the mainland. I made a quick call home for help and my mom sent me recipes from her special folder so I could cook up my favorite dishes.

After school, I returned to my island home for a couple of years before meeting and falling in love with my boyfriend, Moses, a Kailua boy living in San Francisco. It was a Hawai'i boy who took me away from the islands again. When I moved to the Bay Area with Moses, I worked at Williams Sonoma, coordinating all the photography for the company's website. I spent my nights and weekends baking my favorite treats, packaging them up, and gifting them to my coworkers. I loved surprising them and genuinely reveled in bringing delight to others through food. In the spring of 2014, the director of sourcing and product development pulled me into his office and demanded that I tell him what I wanted to do with my "gift." The thing was, I had already begun to consider diving deeper into food on my own terms. A year before, Moses had gifted me a gorgeous set of classic cookbooks and the domain name of FixFeastFlair.com. The site had sat idle until that conversation, and that night I went home and officially started my food blog, *Fix Feast Flair*, where I'm able to share a part of myself and my love for the culinary world with others.

As I became more comfortable with blogging, I began to share recipes from my childhood, thinking that these would be posts that were more for me than my readers. What surprised me was that people really gravitated to those local Hawai'i recipes; perhaps my own love for this food was coming through in my writing and recipes. Around the same time, I started to see more and more recipes pop up on blogs for "Hawaiian" dishes. Recipes such as "Hawaiian Pizza," "Hawaiian Fried Rice," and "Hawaiian Sliders." And that was about the time when I started to think long and hard about writing a book about local Hawai'i food, because here's the thing: just because (and maybe especially because) a dish has pineapple doesn't mean it's Hawaiian.

I understand why people commonly view the duo of pineapple and ham as being from the islands. In the 1950s and 1960s, the advertising campaign of the Hawai'i Visitors Bureau, Hawai'i hotels, and pineapple companies, like Dole and Del Monte, was to brand anything associated with pineapple as "Hawaiian." And the campaign was clearly successful because its effects are still felt today. However, the idea that most people think of ham and pineapple when they think of the food in Hawai'i crushes my heart a little. Don't get me wrong; the sweet and savory dynamic duo of ham and pineapple is great, but it's not Hawaiian. The food I'm exploring in this book is much closer to what I think of as Hawaiian, reflecting how I, my friends, and my family eat when we are at home.

What kind of food is this? It's the superfine, lighter-than-air, rainbow-colored shave ice piled high with mochi balls and with ice cream on the bottom—always ice cream on the bottom—that I ate every Sunday after weekly hula performances. It's the way the house smelled when my mom made Portuguese bean soup and cornbread on a cold day. It's the mouth-puckering, ice-cold pickled mango from Pukalani Superette, the kind that makes your mouth twist up and salivate just thinking about it. It's my uncle's poke, a raw fish salad of sorts, served with hot white rice and ice-cold beers. It's these memories, the memories attached to taste and smell, to local food, that take me home. The local food of Hawai'i, which for the sake of place I will refer to as local Hawai'i food, is a large piece of the heart and soul of the islands.

So what is local Hawai'i food? Simply put, it's a creole cuisine built on the many influences of Hawai'i's early immigrants. It's this beautiful, delicious amalgamation of Hawai'i's migration history that you can see, smell, and, of course, taste. It's the food that locals—you know, the folks who live in Hawai'i—make at home, grab to go in the form of a plate lunch, eat at local fairs, and bring with them to potluck parties and picnics. It's the food that we serve at a baby's first birthday or a wedding. Basically, it's the food that locals have grown up eating.

You might be surprised to find that cozy dishes such as chili, stew, soups, and braised meats are all part of the local Hawai'i food culture. Maybe you've picked up a local Hawai'i cookbook in the past, scanned the table of contents, and thought to yourself, "When do you make this dish? Is it a snack, a main course, or, gosh, is it dessert?" Or maybe you're shocked by the ethnically diverse portfolio of foods and have wondered, "How did all this food get here!?"

To understand how all-encompassing Hawai'i's food culture is, you first have to trace your way through Hawai'i's history. Hawai'i's unique food culture has been greatly influenced by three major diasporas that all ended in Hawai'i. With each wave of settlers, new plants, animals, ingredients, and dishes were introduced and folded into the local food culture. Local Hawai'i food is a direct result of Hawai'i's past and continues to be a living, breathing expression of what Hawai'i is today. In some ways, to understand local Hawai'i food is to understand Hawai'i itself.

LOCAL HAWAI'I FOOD

It is worth noting that while the plantation laborers brought their own unique flavors, ingredients, and dishes to Hawai'i, they were initially just that, their own. Chinese laborers preferred Chinese foods and ingredients; the same was true for the Japanese, the Portuguese, the Koreans, and the Filipinos, each group self-identifying. This segregation of cultures was in part due to the hierarchical caste system that plantation owners worked hard to enforce. They prevented the workers from organizing, dividing the camps based on ethnicity. Eventually, out of necessity, a common language emerged.

Known as Hawaiian Pidgin English, or simply pidgin, this creole language, a hybrid of Hawaiian, English, Chinese, Japanese, and Portuguese, served as a means of communication among all of the groups. While the language allowed for communication on the plantations, it also helped to promote a transfer of knowledge, traditions,

and, yes, food among various groups. Some might even say that it was the catalyst for today's local Hawai'i food culture. With the emergence of pidgin, previously separate groups, divided by language, cultures, beliefs, and even camps, were able to come together through the common denominator of a shared language. The groups of laborers found commonalities once they were able to communicate.

Like pidgin, local Hawai'i food is a hybrid of the many ethnic groups on the plantations. It is not uncommon to find Japanese food served at the same restaurant or party as Filipino and Chinese food. You can get a plate of chili at the same spot that serves Spam musubi and saimin. Just like pidgin, you can't assign just one ethnic group to local Hawai'i food; it's the combination that makes it what it is.

FAMILY HISTORY AND RECIPES

While it may seem like this history is just that—history—it's much more than that to most families in Hawaiʻi, including my own.

Both sets of great-grandparents on my mother's side left Japan for the Big Island of Hawaiʻi in search of a better life. Those great-grandparents were from Yamaguchi, Kumamoto, and Hiroshima. Both of my great-grandfathers worked on the sugar plantations, and over the years, my mother has told me many of our family stories about how hard those days were. After fulfilling his labor contract and working his way up to a supervisor role on the plantation, my great-grandfather on my grandma's side went on to open a saimin and pastry shop with my great-grandmother, which later became Iwata Bakery. They were famous for their fresh coconut pie. My great-grandfather on my grandpa's side left the fields and set up a fish and vegetable delivery business.

Prior to World War II, my grandfather worked as a carpenter. During the war, he served in the 442nd Infantry Regiment. When he got back to Hawaiʻi, he returned to carpentry until he started working as a field supervisor for Hawaiʻi's first commercial papaya farm, Puna Plantation, later renamed Puna Fruit Packers. He worked his way up to vice president of the company, all the while encouraging the workers to become growers. This lead to the formation of Mr. Papaya Co-op, where my grandpa served as general manager and where he got his nickname, Mr. Papaya. His Mr. Papaya Co-op helped open up the markets to Hawaiʻi-grown Solo papayas in the mainland United States and Japan. My grandmother worked as a postal clerk at the Pahoa post office. Their stories and struggles could have only happened in Hawaiʻi; they made my story possible, and I am forever grateful.

To that end, the recipes you'll find in this book stem from family recipes. I've adapted them to my tastes and tinkered with them so that they're as accessible as possible and can be made anywhere in the world. I've offered substitutions or nixed difficult-to-source items whenever possible. However, I feel like I need to make a disclaimer here: Family recipes differ from one to the next, just as each family in Hawaiʻi is different from the one next door. Every family has its own recipe for each of these dishes. The way my mom's beef stew tastes is invariably different from my friend Kammy's dad's beef stew. The same can be said for all the recipes in this book: they are from my experience of Hawaiʻi and all it offers, and they could have only come from a life spent there.

REGIONS OF INFLUENCE

I'm not a historian, but in the case of Hawai'i, context and history are paramount in understanding the local food culture of today. So let's do a quick (I promise!) dive back into Hawai'i's past. While there are other ethnic groups that immigrated to Hawai'i and have contributed to the food culture today, for the purposes of this book, and speaking to the recipes I know best, I will be focusing on the groups listed here. Use the corresponding symbols from each group to identify the origins of the recipes throughout the book.

HAWAIIANS AD 300 to 500

It is generally accepted that Polynesian wayfinders voyaged to the Hawaiian Islands in their double-hulled canoes sometime between AD 300 and 500. Can you imagine what they felt when they saw the beautiful, previously uninhabited island chain we know as Hawai'i? The Polynesian settlers arrived in waves, first coming from the Marquesas Islands and later from Tahiti. And while they found the islands to be abundant in fresh water, fish and shellfish, limu, and birds, there were few edible plants, apart from some ferns and fruits. This is why it's a good thing they brought more than twenty-four plant species, commonly referred to today as canoe plants, as well as chickens, dogs, and pigs. The canoe plants included niu (coconut), kalo (taro), 'ulu (breadfruit), ko (sugarcane), 'ohi'a 'ai (Hawaiian mountain apple), pia (arrowroot), 'olena (turmeric), 'awapuhi (ginger), 'uala (sweet potato), kukui (candlenut), and mai'a (banana).

The diet of the early Hawaiians centered around taro, a thick and fleshy corm or underground stem, similar to a bulb or tuber. Hawaiians transformed it into poi (page 65) by baking it until it was tender and then pounding it with a bit of water to create a thick and transportable substance called pa'i'ai. From

there, more water was added to create poi. It was a staple food of Hawai'i's earliest settlers and is still a mainstay in today's local diet. In addition to poi, the early Hawaiian diet was abundant in seafood and land birds, while also incorporating the many canoe plants brought over to the islands, like sweet potatoes. All of these foods were seasoned with sea salt and served with inamona, a condiment made of roasted and mashed kukui nut meat and sea salt. Limu, a fresh, crunchy, dark, branch-like seaweed, also called ogo, was added to many dishes too.

Pigs were typically reserved for special occasions, to be cooked and offered as religious sacrifice or served at celebrations. These festivities were called pā'ina or 'aha'aina, and today we mostly call them lū'au, named after the lū'au stew, or squid lū'au (page 134), that was served at most of these gatherings. The pigs were cooked in an imu, or earthen oven, along with the taro root, sweet potatoes, and more. This method of cooking the pig, called kālua, steamed and roasted the meat at the same time. It also allowed Hawaiians to cook large quantities of food at once, while keeping it all warm for multiple days. This method of cooking is still used today, and

kālua pig (page 83) is served at many lū'au for baby's first birthdays, graduations, and even weddings.

In the fifteenth century, Chief Mā'ilikūkahi created a system of dividing up parcels of land, from sky to sea, called ahupua'a, to promote productivity. The boundaries of ahupua'a were sometimes marked by ahu, or heaps of altar stones, and/or a pua'a, or wooden pig head, though many had natural markers, like streams or a row of trees. The plots varied in size, with some as small as one hundred acres and some as large as one hundred thousand acres. By sectioning off the land into smaller sections, the people had access to enough food and materials to live comfortably, but not more than they could manage. And what they could not find in their ahupua'a, they were able to get from trading.

WESTERNERS 1778

In 1778, British explorer Captain James Cook and his crew landed at Waimea Bay on Kaua'i. They were the first Europeans to make contact with the Hawaiian Islands. Ram goat, ewe, boar, English sow, melons, pumpkins, and onions were all introduced to the islands at this time. It's also during this time that the name "Sandwich Isles," after the Earl of Sandwich, was given to the island chain by Cook. In 1793, British Captain George Vancouver introduced cattle to the island, gifting California longhorns to King Kamehameha I. Because the cattle faced no natural predators, they multiplied rapidly until the king brought in American John Parker to wrangle and domesticate them. It's at this time that beef becomes a part of the Hawaiian cuisine. The Kamehameha dynasty reigned over Hawai'i from 1795 to 1874, with King Kamehameha I uniting the islands in 1810.

In 1813, Don Francisco de Paula Marín, a Spanish botanist and advisor to King Kamehameha I, cultivated the first pineapple on the island of O'ahu. He cultivated many other crops, including citrus, white potatoes, tomatoes, various types of cabbage, and legumes. Soon after the first European contact, American immigration began, and by 1820, the first Protestant missionaries from the United States arrived in Hawai'i. These immigrants led the efforts to cultivate sugar in the islands, and the first sugar plantation, the Old Sugar Mill, was established by Ladd & Company on Kauai in 1835.

Crews of sailors also made their way to the islands at this time, seeking fortune and glory by way of the whaling industry. The whaling sailors created a demand for fresh fruit, cattle, white potatoes (instead of the sweet potatoes the Hawaiians ate), and sugar. The native Hawaiians grew and supplied these items, while the Europeans and Americans, herein referred to as Westerners, acted as merchants, managing the sale of goods and reaping the majority of the profits. The whaling industry lasted for about forty years, until it came to an abrupt end due to drastic overhunting. In terms of culinary contributions, the whalers introduced salted salmon to the Hawaiians, which was then turned into lomi salmon (page 59).

Soon after the first sugar plantation opened in 1835, sugar and pineapple production exploded. As the plantations started exporting pineapple and producing sugar on a large scale, the American plantation owners found that the labor-intensive farming required a substantially larger workforce. The problem was Westerners had not only introduced new foods to Hawai'i but also new diseases that devastated the local Hawaiians. By the 1840s, the Hawaiian population was less than a sixth of its precontact size, decreasing from 683,000 to fewer than 100,000 by 1845. Many Hawaiians also didn't see the appeal of plantation life, knowing they could instead live off the land by fishing and farming their own crops. These two factors coupled to lead to a new wave of immigration.

CHINESE 1850

In 1850, the first group of Chinese workers came to the islands from Canton (now known as Guangzhou) in Guangdong Province to work as laborers on sugar plantations. Between 1852 and 1887, around 50,000 Chinese traveled to Hawai'i to work in the fields. Around 38 percent of those workers returned to China when their five-year contracts ended, while the rest chose to stay in the islands. New issues arose when Chinese workers immigrated to solve the labor shortage, as they did not live off the land like the native Hawaiians and needed not only food but shelter. They also hungered for the familiar foods and flavors of China, which created a demand for white rice and new herbs and spices.

With the declining Hawaiian population, taro patches were left vacant, and the Chinese turned many of these patches into rice paddies. By the

1860s, rice was on its way to becoming one of the biggest crops in Hawai'i, and by 1888, more than thirteen million pounds of rice were exported to California, making the crop second only to sugar.

The newly established Chinese began to import new varieties of fish, herbs, and spices from their homeland. They introduced many Cantonese dishes to the islands. Stir-fried dishes like chow fun (page 148) and fried rice (page 89) with Chinese-style meats like char siu pork (page 86) are found all over the islands. Dim sum like fried wontons (page 41) and manapua (page 197) are common pūpū and snacks. And li hing mui, or crack-seed-infused, treats, like li hing pickled mango (page 194) and li hing gummy bears (page 202), have all made their way into the local food culture of today's Hawai'i. Many Chinese cultural elements, like Chinese New Year, which includes lion dancing, the gifting of red money envelopes (lai see), and snacking on festive treats like gau (page 186), remain strong today.

JAPANESE 1868

In 1868, the first group of Japanese laborers, known as gannenmono or "first year folks," as that was the first year (gannen) of the Meiji period in Japan, arrived in the islands. However, it wasn't until 1885, after the Japanese government legalized immigration to Hawai'i in the form of "contract labor" as part of a larger deal to access rice at a low and fair price, that the first large group of Japanese contract laborers arrived in Hawai'i, ushering in a giant wave of Japanese workers. By 1924, around 200,000 Japanese laborers, mainly from Yamaguchi, Hiroshima, Fukuoka City, and Kumamoto, had arrived to work in the pineapple and sugar fields, with around 55 percent returning to Japan when their contracts ended.

Like the Chinese that came before them, the Japanese hungered for the foods and traditions of their homeland. After the initial wave, they brought seeds to plant familiar produce, and by 1900, the Japanese communities were growing kabocha squash, daikon, lettuces, green onions, string beans, Japanese eggplant, turnips, gobo (burdock root), and shiso. It is said that you could see the kabocha squash growing around and up onto the shacks of the Japanese laborers. In 1908, the first sake brewery outside of Japan opened in Honolulu.

Many dishes were introduced to Hawai'i by the Japanese. The iconic shave ice (page 172) is said to have originated from the Japanese kakigōri. Japanese bentos, sashimi, tofu, and soy sauce (shoyu) are all a part of today's local Hawai'i food culture. Steaming, broiling, simmering, and frying methods that were implemented by the early immigrants as a means of cooking without an oven (a luxury early laborers did not have) remain popular today in the form of teriyaki beef sticks (page 119) and fried reef fish (page 136). The love of pickled veggies (see takuan, page 69, and namasu, page 68) also continues. And mochi is as beloved as ever (see butter mochi, page 167). Japanese Obon festivals that celebrate the spirits of one's ancestors are popular with locals, as are the foods and traditions of special occasions like New Year, when you will find kagami mochi, which is a tower of two round mochi with a tangerine on top, and kadomatsum, made of pine and bamboo pieces, in local grocery stores.

PORTUGUESE 1878

The first Portuguese immigrants came to Hawai'i from the Azores and Madeira. Later groups came over from Portugal and Cape Verde. Over the course of about thirty years, more than 16,000 Portuguese immigrants arrived in the islands to work the plantations. While most of the other immigrant groups arrived as single men or women, the Portuguese typically came over as families, with the intention of staying in Hawaiʻi. The Portuguese were offered better working conditions, contracts, and oftentimes worked as luna, or supervisors, instead of laborers. When their work contracts ended, some Portuguese opened up bakeries and restaurants, while many became paniolo (cowboys), working on the cattle ranches.

In terms of food, the Portuguese immigrants brought with them their love for pork, tomatoes, and chili peppers, as well as oven-baked breads like pão doce, aka Portuguese sweet bread (page 191). You can see their influence on the local Hawaiʻi food culture with dishes like Portuguese bean soup (page 97), cornbread (page 74), Portuguese sausage (page 73), and malasadas (page 183). In addition to their influence on the food culture, the Portuguese introduced both the ʻukulele and the style of strumming that would be instrumental in the creation of the steel guitar, a gift that is still heard today.

KOREANS 1903

The first Korean laborers came over in 1903 from the port city of Incheon to work on the plantations. More than 7,500 Koreans arrived between the years 1903 and 1910, with only 16 percent of the laborers returning to Korea. The 1900 Hawaiian Organic Act banned contract labor, so unlike the Chinese and Japanese who came before them, the Koreans were not locked into long-term contracts. This impacted their lives greatly, as they did not spend much time on the plantations and instead moved on to other types of work much more quickly than the groups that preceded them.

Kim chee (page 70) and barbecued marinated meats, like kalbi (page 120), are two of the largest Korean contributions to local Hawaiʻi food. Pickled vegetables like namul exist today, as well as egg-battered meat jun (page 123) and spicy condiments like gochujang.

FILIPINOS 1906

In 1906, the first Filipino plantation laborers arrived; most were male and unmarried. At the peak of the sugar production, more than half of the workforce was composed of Filipino laborers. By 1930, more than 112,000 Filipinos had come, and about 65 percent stayed on the islands. Most of the early waves of Filipino laborers came from the Ilocos region and the Visayas. As one of the later groups of plantation laborers to make their way to Hawaiʻi, they found it much easier to import the ingredients they longed for. They brought with them peas and beans, vinegar, and garlic-based dishes, and preferred to boil, stew, broil, and fry foods (like many of the other laborers who came before them). Filipino dishes like pork adobo (page 107) and cascaron (page 180) are cornerstones of Hawaiʻi's local food culture today.

Although there aren't any recipes in this book tied to Okinawa or Puerto Rico, both groups have played a role in the development of local Hawaiʻi food. The first Okinawan and Puerto Rican plantation workers arrived in Hawaiʻi in 1900. Today, there are more than 50,000 ethnic Okinawans and 35,000 ethnic Puerto Ricans in Hawaiʻi.

JOURNEY TO STATEHOOD

Now that you've explored the various ethnic groups and what they brought to Hawai'i and its food, it's important also to get a sense of Hawai'i's political past and how it went from a kingdom ruled by a sovereign monarchy to the fiftieth state of the United States of America.

1810 King Kamehameha I, also known as Kamehameha the Great, unites the Hawaiian Islands.

1819 Liholiho, son of Kamehameha I, abolishes the kapu (taboo) system. Part of this system is the tradition of men and women eating separately during feasts.

1839 The Hawaiian Bill of Rights, also known as the 1839 Constitution of Hawai'i, is signed into law. King Kamehameha III, born Kauikeaouli, and his chiefs attempted to keep the lands in the hands of the Hawaiian people by providing them with the groundwork for a free enterprise system.

1840 The 1840 Constitution of the Kingdom of Hawai'i is signed into law. With this constitution, Kamehameha III established a constitutional monarchy that stated that the land belonged to the people and was to be managed by the king. According to the constitution, the lands were to be divided into thirds, one-third to the Hawaiian crown, one-third to the chiefs, and one-third to the Hawaiian people. However, this law required land claims to be filed within two years. Less than 1 percent of the Hawaiian people filed claims, as land ownership seemed odd to Hawaiians, who didn't believe that nature could be owned. The Great Māhele "to divide or portion" ultimately had the opposite effect of its intent, as most of the land was eventually sold to the Big Five corporations, which controlled the sugar industry and many related businesses in Hawai'i, leaving little in the hands of Hawai'i and its people.

1874 King Kamehameha VI, born Lunalilo, also known as "the People's King," dies, leaving no heirs and thus ending the reign for the Kamehameha dynasty. King David Kalākaua is elected as his successor.

1882 'Iolani Palace, the home of Hawaiian monarchs, is completed. It's outfitted with the first electric lights in Hawai'i, indoor plumbing, and a telephone. This is quite a feat, as not even the White House or Buckingham Palace was decked out in these amenities at that time.

1887 The 1887 Constitution of the Kingdom of Hawai'i, also known as the Bayonet Constitution, is signed. King Kalākaua is forcibly coerced into signing the law that handed power over to the legislature and the cabinet, stripping it away from the monarchy.

1891 King Kalākaua dies. Hawai'i's first queen and last monarch, Queen Lili'uokalani, sister of King Kalākaua, takes the throne.

1893 Queen Lili'uokalani is placed under house arrest and the overthrow of the Kingdom of Hawai'i starts.

1898 Through a joint resolution, the Newlands Resolution, the United States annexes Hawai'i.

1900 Hawai'i becomes the Territory of Hawai'i with the Hawaiian Organic Act.

1917 Queen Lili'uokalani, the Kingdom of Hawai'i's last sovereign, dies.

1941 On December 7, 1941, the Japanese attack Pearl Harbor, on O'ahu, during World War II.

1959 On August 21, 1959, by popular vote, Hawai'i becomes the fiftieth state of the United States of America.

1978 Hawaiian is made Hawai'i's official language by the Hawai'i State Constitutional Convention. Hawai'i becomes the only state in the United States to have a non-English official language.

2009 Hawai'i-born senator Barack Obama is inaugurated as the forty-fourth president of the United States.

ANATOMY OF A PLATE LUNCH

People like to call Hawaiʻi the ultimate cultural melting pot, while others argue it's more like a salad bowl. I, however, believe that it's like a really good mixed plate.

If you're still looking to understand what local Hawaiʻi food is like, look no further than the plate lunch. From doctors to surfers to your aunty down the street, it's fair to say that most locals eat plate lunches. You can find them almost anywhere, from lunch wagons to delis (Hawaiʻi-style delis, that is, which do not serve smoked fish and bagels and might not even serve sandwiches), drive-ins, diners, and hole-in-the-wall restaurants. You can get them at local restaurant chains, like Zippy's. Even former president Barack Obama has been known to frequent spots such as Rainbow Drive-In and Zippy's to get his plate lunch fix.

Mayo-y Carbohydrate

Carbohydrate

Vegetable

Protein

SO WHAT IS A PLATE LUNCH AND HOW DID IT COME TO BE?

A plate lunch typically consists of three, sometimes four, items: protein, carbohydrate, mayo-y carbohydrate, and possibly a vegetable (though it's likely pickled). It's usually served on a sectioned plate or container, hence plate lunch. What makes it so special is that it's a true representation of Hawai'i's local food culture and the ethnically diverse population. You can actually see all the different groups represented on the menu at any plate lunch spot. From Japanese teriyaki beef to Filipino chicken adobo to Korean kalbi short ribs, everyone is represented.

While no one knows definitively when or where the plate lunch was born, one story goes something like this. Plantation workers carried their lunches in bento boxes or tins, also called kau kau (food) tins. Lunch usually consisted of leftover white rice with a combination of the following: leftover meats, canned meats, scrambled eggs, and pickled vegetables. By the 1930s, lunch wagons set up shop, selling plates that consisted of similar foods, with the addition of mac salad (page 55) and sometimes potatoes.

PROTEIN

The focal point of the plate lunch is the protein. When you order a plate lunch, you're essentially ordering according to which protein you're in the mood for. The mixed plate is for when you're feeling indecisive and want to pick two, sometimes three, different proteins. Below are some examples of popular menu items, but this list is by no means exhaustive.

Chicken Katsu (page 111)

Kālua Pig (page 83)

Beef Stew (page 127)

Pork Laulau (page 78)

Local-Style BBQ Chicken (page 108)

Shoyu Chicken (page 103)

Chicken Adobo (page 107)

Mochiko Chicken (page 100)

Teriyaki Beef Sticks (page 119)

Maui-Style Kalbi Short Ribs (page 120)

Beef Curry (page 124)

Squid Lū'au (page 134)

Pork and Peas (page 94)

Ginger Misoyaki Butterfish (page 139)

Loco Moco (page 115)

CARBOHYDRATE

A carbohydrate is the cornerstone of every plate lunch: one or (more commonly) two scoops of steamed white rice. And yes, the rice is usually scooped into half spherical mounds with a big ice cream scooper. If you're feeling health conscious, you might ask for brown rice. If you're feeling only a little health conscious, you might ask for hapa rice, which is half brown rice, half white rice. And while it's almost sacrilegious, I have heard a few people order and ask for no rice, but that usually leads to some raised eyebrows.

MAYO-Y CARBOHYDRATE

This is not the technical name, but like it or not, mac (short for macaroni) salad or potato mac salad (page 55) is basically just that: a mayo-y carbohydrate. You usually just get one scoop of this. If the protein is the quarterback of the plate, the mayo-y carbohydrate is a member of the offensive line. A good mac salad is more than just macaroni and mayonnaise. It's got tang, a bit of bite (thank you, onion), and a touch of sweetness. I think you can tell a lot about a place by its mac salad.

VEGETABLE

One of three scenarios plays out here. Usually, there's no vegetable. Sometimes, there's a pickled vegetable like kim chee (page 70), takuan (page 69), or namasu (page 68). Less likely is the third scenario, which is a tossed salad of sorts, usually dressed with a papaya seed dressing (page 218) or a creamy Asian dressing (page 217). Most plate lunches aren't about the veggies, though I can't say no plate lunches have veggies 'cause that's just not true. There's a spot in Diamond Head on O'ahu called Diamond Head Market & Grill, and its plate lunches come with a "toss" salad.

THE BASICS

At the end of the day, I want this book to become yours. I want you to cook from it the way you choose. There's no right or wrong way to use this book, but here are some notes and suggestions on how to get the most out of it. The paper is something that you might not give a second thought to, but I selected it specifically to allow for notes, for years of wear, for the stains of history to soak in. I've included menu suggestions for each recipe, as inspiration to build a complete meal or plate lunch. So take out a pen or pencil and get to cooking!

If you look at a recipe and think, "That's not nearly enough salt," or "Whoa, too much paprika!" jot down those notes. If you absolutely can't stand fish sauce, strike it out. If you grew up adding peas to your fried rice, add those peas! I am not here to make cooking frustrating, difficult, or even challenging. You can adjust all the recipes to your liking. The point of this book is to give you a starting point, a base recipe. Choose your own adventure here and make these recipes your own! Or don't and leave them the way they are if you love them! And remember, your cooktop and oven will vary from mine, so don't forget that and adjust your times and temps accordingly. I want you to fall in love with local Hawai'i food the way I have, and the only way to do that is to welcome it into your kitchen. My hope is that every dish you make will transport you to the islands.

A note on orthography and diacritical marks. You may find familiar dishes and ingredients spelled differently than you are accustomed. No, that's not a typo on kim chee. In Hawai'i's orthography, you'll find many words spelled phonetically; to stay true to Hawai'i's local food culture, the spellings (or misspellings in some cases) must be observed. There are two diacritical marks in the Hawaiian language: The ', or 'okina, is a glottal stop, like the hyphen between "uh-oh." And the macron above vowels, like ō, is a kahakō, and it lengthens and stresses the marked vowel.

BUILDING BLOCKS

I'm not a classically trained chef—I'm a home cook. Still, over the years, I've learned a few tips and tricks that have made life in the kitchen a lot easier. If you're reading this book, I'll assume that you have at least a baseline level of cooking knowledge, and if you don't, that's cool too. We all have to start somewhere, right? Here are some general guides and a few things I wish I had learned when I was just starting out.

KNIFE SKILLS 101

I hold my knife by gripping the top of the blade between my thumb and index finger and wrapping the rest of my fingers around the handle. To me, it allows for better control and the easiest cutting, but you should hold your knife however feels most natural.

Minced = chopped into very small pieces; think smaller than a piece of short-grain rice

Chopped = chopped into small pieces; think bigger than a piece of short-grain rice, smaller than ½-inch squares

Diced = chopped into ½-inch squares

Cubed = chopped into ¾- to 1-inch squares; think bite-size cubes

Sliced = cut into slices

Julienned = thin, matchstick-like cuts, usually 2 to 3 inches long. To achieve this, you slice the item into thin sheets, then stack those sheets and cut them into thin sticks.

Shredded = cut into thin strips, usually cabbage or other leafy greens

Finely grated = use a fine Microplane grater

Grated = use the small holes of a box grater

Coarsely grated = use the big holes of a box grater

When you are chopping leafy things like herbs, sprinkle a little salt on them to keep them from wiggling around.

To keep your cutting board in place, try putting a wet paper towel under the board. Voilà! No more dancing board.

To clean your cutting board, sprinkle Hawaiian salt ('alaea) all over it, then rub it with half a lemon. The acid from the lemon will disinfect and deodorize it, and the salt will rub off all the tiny bits of crud.

PEELING

Different produce calls for different methods. Below are the methods that I find easiest.

To peel a garlic clove, use a chef's knife to trim off the hard root, then place the clove on a flat surface and lay your knife flat on it, blade edge away from you. Press down with the heel of your palm until the clove gives a little. The skin should slip right off.

To peel fresh ginger, hold the piece of ginger in your nondominant hand. Hold a teaspoon in your dominant hand, grasping the handle in an almost fist-like gesture and with your thumb on the middle of the convex side of the spoon. With long strokes and gentle pressure, use the tip and bottom edge of the spoon to scrape away the skin.

To peel potatoes, use a paring knife to gently cut a line into the skin around the middle of the potato before boiling. After boiling, the skin should peel right off the potato.

ROOM TEMPERATURE

This is something that often gets overlooked, but if at all possible, it is best to bring your ingredients to room temperature. This is mostly for meats and butter, but I also do it for eggs and veggies. It is best to avoid going from super cold to super hot, or vice versa.

READ AND REREAD

More than once I've made it halfway through a recipe, only to realize I don't have a crucial ingredient. To prevent yourself from making my mistakes, read the recipe all the way through, and then read it again before you start cooking.

MISE IT

Mise en place is a French phrase that roughly translates to "everything in its place," and while you may be tired of hearing about it, we're still talking about it for a reason. Basically, get all your ingredients out and ready to go before you dive in.

BUILDING YOUR PANTRY

If you're new to cooking local Hawai'i food, you're gonna want to take the time to build up your larder with the necessary staples. Nowadays, if you're living on either coast of the United States, or in a community with a large Asian population, you can find most of these items in a local grocery store. However, if you're having trouble finding certain items, head to an Asian grocer or go online! Amazon has made it pretty easy for me to bring Hawai'i home to my Los Angeles kitchen.

I have done my best to eliminate the hard-to-source ingredients whenever possible or to provide substitutions. However, to stay authentic, there are certain instances when this is not possible.

ALCOHOLS

Alcohol is typically used in a marinade or braise to tenderize meats, and ends up cooking off, leaving behind loads of flavor. Store all of these in a cool, dry, dark place.

Mirin is a sweet Japanese cooking sake with a lower alcohol content and more sugar than traditional sake. My favorite brand is Takara Masamune Mirin, produced and bottled by Honolulu Sake Brewing Company Ltd. You can find it in the alcohol section at Whole Foods, near the sakes. If you can't find Takara Masamune Mirin, look for Eden Mirin in the Asian foods section. As a last resort, you can buy Kikkoman Aji-Mirin; however, decrease the sugar in the recipe slightly if you do.

Red wine needs no introduction. But when it comes to cooking with wine, I subscribe to the philosophy that you should always cook with the wine you want to drink. So, grab a bottle of your favorite red, add some to your dish, and then pour a glass for yourself while you're at it.

Sake should be filtered and clear. Do not use a nigori, or unfiltered sake.

Whiskey is similar to wine in that I believe you should use the whiskey you drink. If you don't like whiskey or don't happen to have any on hand, you can substitute brandy or sherry.

BROTHS

Look for a broth in a Tetra Pak (that soft-coated carton near the cans). My favorite brand is Pacific Foods, but Whole Foods 365 and Trader Joe's are both good options. Store them in a cool, dry, dark place.

CANNED GOODS

This probably goes without saying, but look for cans that are BPA-free or buy Tetra Pak goods when you can. Store them in a cool, dry, dark place.

Maybe it's a product of my childhood, but I just prefer canned red kidney beans to dried kidney beans. To each their own, but if you go the canned route, I usually just get organic Whole Foods 365.

I prefer using fresh or frozen coconut milk. However, not everyone has access to it. So if you're using a canned or Tetra Pak coconut milk, look for one with only one or two ingredients: coconut milk and water. Aroy-D Tetra Paks are my favorite. And make sure you're purchasing a culinary coconut milk not a coconut milk beverage, as the latter is much more watery.

Evaporated milk still has a place in a modern kitchen, though it might feel like a relic of the past. It's creamier than regular milk, with about 60 percent less water content. And unlike condensed milk, it has no added sugar.

Spam Less Sodium is the only Spam on hand in my kitchen. It's got 25 percent less sodium than Spam Classic, which, in my opinion, is more than enough.

CHINESE FIVE-SPICE POWDER

This is a spice blend of five or more spices that's used primarily in Chinese cooking. Typically, it's a combination of star anise, cloves, cinnamon, Sichuan pepper, and fennel, but it can also include ginger, anise, nutmeg, turmeric, cardamom, licorice, and mandarin orange peel. Funny enough, the brand that I use, Dynasty, has seven spices: cinnamon, star anise, fennel, ginger, cloves, white pepper, and licorice. Like all spices, store it in a cool, dry place away from direct sunlight. You can find it in the Asian foods section of your grocery store.

CORNSTARCH

Maybe you're surprised to see that cornstarch has made the list, but it is found in many local recipes. Look for a non-GMO cornstarch, like Clabber Girl or Rapunzel. You can substitute arrowroot if you want.

DRIED NOODLES

If you don't know what you're looking for, it's easy to confuse one of these noodles for the other, especially because many of them go by more than one name, depending on whom you're talking to or where you're buying them. They can all be found in the Asian foods section of your grocery store or at an Asian market. If you don't have access to either, they are all available on Amazon.

Somen are thin, white Japanese noodles.

Bean threads, also known as mung bean noodles, cellophane noodles, glass noodles, or long rice (which is confusing, as they are not made with rice), are made from a starch or a mix of starches such as mung bean, arrowroot, cornstarch, tapioca, and/or sweet potato. They are sold in small bunches of fine strands and need to be hydrated before use.

Pancit bihon, also known as rice stick noodles, rice noodles, maifun or bifun, or rice vermicelli, is a very fine noodle that comes bundled similar to bean thread noodles. They, too, need to be hydrated before use.

Pancit canton, also known as wheat stick noodles, is a Cantonese noodle made with wheat flour and sometimes egg. These noodles do not need to be hydrated ahead of time.

FISH SAUCE

Whether you call it nam pla (Thai), nuoc mam (Vietnamese), or patis (Filipino), fish sauce is a common ingredient in many Southeast Asian dishes. It is funky (in the best way possible), salty, and adds incredible depth to dishes. It's literally fermented anchovies, which might sound intimidating, but a little goes a long way, and there really isn't a substitute for it. Can you say umami? You can find it in most grocery stores, either in the Asian foods section or near the soy sauce (shoyu). My favorite brand is Red Boat.

FLOURS

Store your flours in airtight containers in a cool, dry place away from direct sunlight. If stored properly, all of these flours should last one to two years. If it has turned, the flour will smell sour.

All-purpose flour is the standard white flour that you'll find in most kitchens. It has 10 to 11 percent protein, which is pretty much in the middle as far as all flours go. Basically this means about that much gluten will form when the flour comes into contact with water. Look for unbleached all-purpose flour; I like King Arthur Unbleached All-Purpose Flour. If you don't want to commit to buying bread or cake flour, you can substitute all-purpose flour. Bread flour and all-purpose flour can be substituted 1 to 1, while cake flour requires a little more math: 1 cup of cake flour equals 1 cup of all-purpose flour minus 2 tablespoons that are replaced with cornstarch. You won't get quite the same texture when you substitute all-purpose for bread flour, but it'll be close enough.

Bread flour has 11 to 13 percent protein, meaning it will produce more gluten than all-purpose flour and create a chewier end product. Use white bread flour for recipes in this book. King Arthur Bread Flour is the brand I use.

Cake flour has a lower protein content than all-purpose, usually around 9 percent. This basically means less gluten, which means lighter and more tender end results. I use King Arthur Unbleached Cake Flour.

Mochiko is very different from the other three. It roughly translates to "mochi flour" and is made with sweet, or glutinous, rice. It is sometimes called sweet rice flour, which can be slightly confusing, as the flour itself is not sweet, but it is made from sweet rice. Also, it's gluten-free. I use Koda Farms brand.

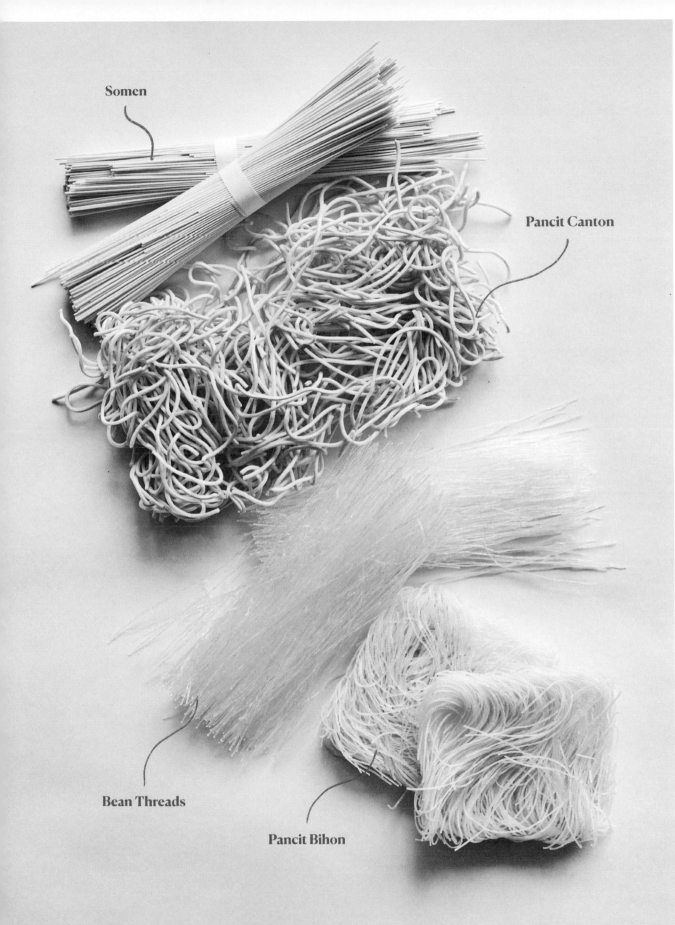

Somen

Pancit Canton

Bean Threads

Pancit Bihon

HONEY

Look for a light-colored, mild honey, like clover or orange. If your honey crystallizes, simply place the bottle in a bath of hot water. The heat should return the honey to its original form.

LI HING MUI AND LI HING POWDER

Li hing mui is a salted dried plum that originated in Guangdong Province, China, and is very popular in Hawai'i today. Sometimes called crack seed, it's sweet, salty, and sour all at the same time. Li hing mui roughly translates to "traveling plum." People in Hawai'i snack on this or grind it up into a powder and sprinkle it on everything from shave ice (page 172) to gummy bears (page 202) to fresh fruits. In its ground form, it's called li hing powder. Look for red li hing mui or li hing mui powder; white doesn't have quite the same flavor. My favorite brand is Jade. Store it in an airtight container the same way you store your spices.

LIQUID SMOKE

Exactly what it sounds like, a liquid that tastes and smells like smoke, liquid smoke is the key to capturing the smoky flavor of an imu at home. A little goes a long way, and if stored properly in a cool, dark place, a small bottle will last for years. I recommend ordering For J's Hawai'i Kiawe Liquid Smoke on Amazon because it uses kiawe (a type of mesquite), which is a common type of firewood in Hawai'i.

MAYONNAISE

The only mayo option is Best Foods, or Hellmann's if you're in the eastern part of the US. It's well balanced, tangy, sweet, salty, rich, creamy. Store it in the refrigerator after opening it.

NUTS AND SEEDS

Store nuts and seeds in a cool, dark, dry place for up to 3 months or in a freezer bag for up to a year. They have a high oil content and go rancid quickly. I toast macadamia nuts and sesame seeds before using, unless they are going into a baked good, in which case the baking process takes care of the toasting. In all my recipes, I use salted dry-roasted macadamia nuts.

I typically reach for roasted white sesame seeds and, to boost the flavor, toast them in a pan on the stove top over low heat briefly before using.

OILS

Store all of your oils in a cool, dark, dry place far away from your oven or stove top. While expiration dates are handy, your nose is your best friend when checking for freshness. You will be able to smell when an oil is rancid. You should be able to find these oils in your grocery store; however, Amazon will have all of them if you can't.

Macadamia oil is more of a finishing oil than a cooking oil, unless you want a lot of macadamia nut flavor; it is very nutty. It will keep for only a few months after it's opened, so I'd recommend buying small amounts at a time.

Neutral oils are mild-flavored oils with high smoke points. Avocado oil, canola oil, and sunflower oil are all neutral oils, and I use them interchangeably. Stored properly, avocado oil can keep for up to 8 months, while canola and sunflower oil should keep for up to a year.

Sesame oils vary greatly from brand to brand. I prefer Kadoya and pick it up at Marukai Market (one of the biggest Japanese supermarkets in the United States; www.tokyocentral.com), but it can also be ordered on Amazon. If you are looking for more nuttiness, try a toasted sesame oil. Sesame oil has a shelf life of about 6 months.

OYSTER SAUCE

Thick, dark, salty oyster sauce is used in a lot of Chinese recipes, such as fried wontons (page 41), stir-fries like fried rice (page 89) and chow fun (page 148), and dishes like stuffed Local-Style Fish (page 137). Store it in your refrigerator. I recommend using Lee Kum Kee premium oyster sauce (the one with the gold foil on the label).

PEPPERS

The only two dried peppers used in this book are black pepper and gochugaru. Black peppercorns should always be freshly ground with a pepper mill, and gochugaru comes flaked. Store both of these in a cool, dry place away from heat.

Black peppercorns, the most common peppercorn, should be purchased whole and ground right before using, as opposed to preground, which loses its flavor quickly.

Gochugaru is a Korean red chili flake. If you don't have it, you can substitute Aleppo pepper, which is a Middle Eastern chili flake. And if all you have on hand is crushed red pepper flakes, you can substitute that, though I'd recommend running it through a spice grinder to break it down a bit.

RICE

I don't have a real statistic for this, but if I had to guess, I'd say at least nine out of ten homes in Hawai'i have a rice cooker and that rice cooker lives on the kitchen counter. When you eat as much rice as people from Hawai'i do, a rice cooker is a worthy investment. I'd highly suggest investing in a Zojirushi rice cooker. The first step to making great rice is to make sure you rinse it until the water runs clear before you cook it. As for types of rice, I'd say that most people use either short-grain white rice or a Calrose or Kokuho Rose medium-grain white rice. The rice is cooked until it's moist and almost sticky (but don't use sticky rice for everyday cooking), and it's never mushy. Store your rice in an airtight container in a cool, dry place away from direct sunlight.

Hapa rice is a combination of half white rice mixed with half brown rice. Hinode even makes a premixed Hapa Blend! However, if you can't find it, don't worry; you can make your own by mixing together equal parts of white and brown rice of the same grain size.

For medium-grain white rice, I recommend Kokuho Rose or Calrose; my favorite brand of rice is Koda Farms. You can find it at Marukai Market or order it through their website if you don't have physical access to a location.

Again, my favorite brand of short-grain white rice is Koda Farms.

SALT

There are only two salts you need in your kitchen Hawaiian salt ('alaea) and kosher salt. Anytime you're not using one, you're using the other. Sometimes you need to use both.

Hawaiian salt, also known as 'alaea, is a coarse sea salt that's been harvested from areas with red alae volcanic clay. Source this salt from Hawai'i. I buy from Hawaiian Pa'akai Inc., which you can find on Amazon. While it's a little more expensive, the flavor is worth it. However, if you cannot find it, substitute a coarse sea salt, like pink Himalayan salt.

The only kosher salt I recommend is Diamond Crystal. The flake is different than that of other kosher salts, it dissolves quickly, and it's less salty and, therefore, more forgiving if you happen to accidentally oversalt a dish.

SHIITAKE MUSHROOMS

I always keep a stock of dried shiitake mushrooms on hand. They add a ton of flavor to any dish. Pick them up in an Asian market, where they are sold in larger quantities for better prices. Store them in an airtight container in a cool, dry spot.

SEAWEED

There are two dried seaweeds that play a large role in Hawai'i's multiethnic cuisine.

Furikake is a Japanese seasoning of dried seaweeds, sesame seeds, salt, sugar, and sometimes dried fish. I like nori komi furikake; always look for Mishima brand. Sprinkle it over everything from rice to popcorn (page 206).

Nori, also called roasted seaweed, is sold in packages of ten sheets. Typically used for sushi, it can also wrap Mochiko Chicken (page 100) or Soy-Glazed Spam Musubi (page 90).

Store them in an airtight container in a cool, dry place. You can find both in the Asian section of your grocery store, at Marukai Market, or online via Pacific East West.

SOY SAUCE

More commonly known as shoyu in Hawai'i, this sauce is made from fermented soybeans. It is packed with umami and salt, which add depth to dishes. I always keep a cooking soy sauce and a finishing (lighter, less sodium) soy sauce on hand.

Kikkoman is a good, all-purpose soy sauce. It's in the midrange as far as saltiness and strength of flavor go (in the wide spectrum of soy sauces).

Aloha shoyu is what I like to refer to as my finishing soy sauce. It's lighter than most and adds just a touch of salt and umami to a dish. I always keep a bottle out for people to add at their own discretion.

SUGAR

With Hawai'i's history of sugar production, it's no surprise that sugar plays a large role in most dishes. There are two cane sugars I always keep on hand. Store both in airtight containers, in—yes, you guessed it—a cool, dry place away from direct sunlight. I use C&H (California and Hawaiian Sugar Company) brand.

Brown sugar is available in light and dark varieties—your call here, but I usually use only dark brown sugar. It has more molasses, so the flavor is just a little stronger. A fun trick to softening your crystallized brown sugar: Place a piece of bread in the sugar container for 24 hours. The sugar will soak up all the moisture from the bread.

Granulated sugar, with its neutral flavor and fine crystal texture, is something that is so recognizable that there is no substitute for it. From savory to sweet dishes, this is a kitchen staple that really works hard.

VINEGAR

Acidity is a building block in recipes that's often overlooked. While vinegar is commonly associated with things such as salad dressings and pickles, when it's added to soups, marinades, and braises, it really shines. It boosts flavors and complexity, lending balance to dishes. While cane vinegar and rice vinegar aren't the only two vinegars in my local Hawai'i food pantry, if I had to pick two, I'd pick cane vinegar and rice vinegar. As with most things, store your vinegars in a cool, dry, dark place.

Cane vinegar is not sweet, even though it's made from sugarcane syrup. It's mellower than distilled white vinegar and can be substituted for champagne vinegar, cider vinegars, and white wine vinegar. I buy Datu Puti brand from Amazon.

Rice vinegar, made from fermented rice, is very light and mild; I add it to most things. I usually buy a large bottle of Mizkan from Marukai or a few bottles of Kikkoman from Whole Foods.

WATER

I always use filtered or purified water when cooking. While tap water is an option, I feel like it sometimes introduces new flavors that aren't ideal.

WORCESTERSHIRE SAUCE

I like to call this the "everything sauce," as it has so many ingredients, from vinegar to anchovies. It's a thin, dark-colored sauce that adds tons of depth to any dish. Store in the refrigerator after opening it.

PRODUCE GUIDE

Many of these items can be found in your local market or Asian market almost year-round, but some have specific seasons. A few, like pohole fern, lūʻau, and nīoi, may be harder to find outside of Hawaiʻi, but substitutions have been suggested whenever possible.

Baby Bok Choy firm stalks, tender leaves, sweet

Banana Leaves pliable, aromatic, large

Bean Sprouts (sometimes called mung bean sprouts) crisp, crunchy, mild

Cabbage, Green or Red sturdy, smooth leaves, crunchy

Cilantro delicate leaves, citrus, bright

Coconut fragrant, mildly oily, mildly sweet

Daikon (sometimes called white, long, or winter radish) crisp, juicy, mild

Garlic pungent, spicy, strong

Ginger aromatic, spicy, pungent

Green Onions (aka scallions) sweet, mild, crunchy

Guava sweet and very fragrant, dense texture, moderately acidic

Hawaiian Chili Peppers (nīoi) hot, small, similar to thai chili

Lilikoʻi (passion fruit) pineapple-y tart, berrylike flavor, very aromatic

Maui Onion sweet and mild flavor, crispy, juicy

Napa Cabbage (Won Bok) thick stems, frilly leaves, sweet

Okinawan Sweet Potato sweet, purple, chestnut notes

Pohole Fern (also called ostrich fern, warabi, hoʻiʻo, kosade, or pako) crunchy outside like asparagus, nutty, slimy inside like okra

Solo Papaya sweet with distinct smell, melony flavor, soft flesh

Taro (kalo or lūʻau) Leaves subtle, slightly nutty, varies in size

Taro (kalo) Root starchy, meaty, mildly sweet

Ti Leaves pliable, aromatic, small

Watercress peppery, mustardy, delicate leaves

Baby Bok Choy

Daikon

Hawaiian Chili Peppers

Solo Papaya

Banana Leaves

Liliko'i

Taro Leaves

Bean Sprouts

Garlic

Maui Onion

Taro Root

Cabbage, Green or Red

Ginger

Napa Cabbage

Ti Leaves

Cilantro

Green Onions

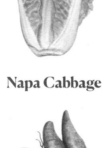

Okinawan Sweet Potato

Coconut

Guava

Pohole Fern

Watercress

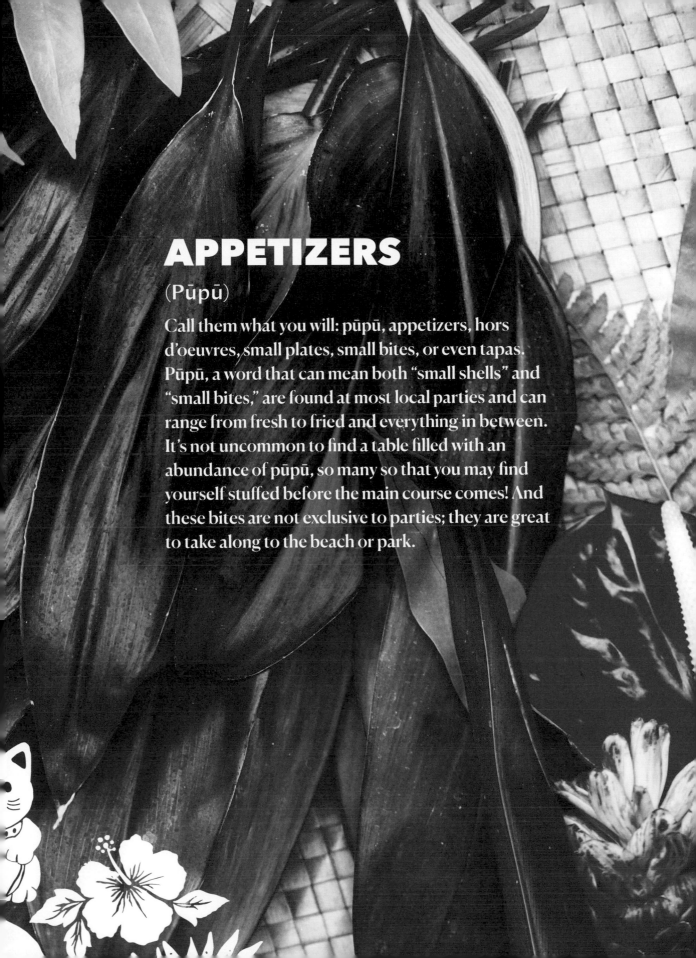

APPETIZERS

(Pūpū)

Call them what you will: pūpū, appetizers, hors d'oeuvres, small plates, small bites, or even tapas. Pūpū, a word that can mean both "small shells" and "small bites," are found at most local parties and can range from fresh to fried and everything in between. It's not uncommon to find a table filled with an abundance of pūpū, so many so that you may find yourself stuffed before the main course comes! And these bites are not exclusive to parties; they are great to take along to the beach or park.

SHOYU 'AHI POKE

1 pound fresh sashimi-grade 'ahi steak, chilled and cut into 1-inch cubes

1½ tablespoons soy sauce (shoyu), plus more to taste

1 tablespoon sesame oil

¾ teaspoon Hawaiian salt ('alaea), plus more to taste

¼ cup thinly sliced Maui or yellow onion

½ cup chopped green onions, green parts only

⅛ teaspoon gochugaru (see page 30)

1 tablespoon finely chopped toasted macadamia nuts

2 cups steamed rice, for serving

Serves 2 to 4

ON THE MENU:

Pickled Onion, page 67
Kālua Pig, page 83
Haupia, page 168

It seems like there are new, flavor-packed poke spots popping up on every corner of Los Angeles, New York, and San Francisco, but in Hawai'i, simplicity is king. The fresh, raw fish is meant to be the shining star of the dish. When I was in my early twenties, I lived in Honolulu. After a long day of work, I'd grab a tub of poke from Tamura's Liquor and Fine Wine on Waialae Avenue, one of the best places in the city for poke, and a couple of ice-cold Japanese beers. From there, I'd go home, grab Vienna (my dog), a towel, and a friend, and we'd spend the evening at the beach with our pūpū (aka appetizers) and refreshments while we watched the sun go down.

Poke literally translates to "section" or "to slice or cut," so it makes sense that it's the name of a dish that's basically just cubes of beautiful raw fish. The most common type of fish used is 'ahi, or yellowfin tuna, but no matter what, you want the freshest fish you can possibly find. Ask your fish guy for sashimi- or sushi-grade cuts, tell him you're making poke, and chances are he'll hook you up with the best fish he's got.

In a bowl, combine the cubed 'ahi, soy sauce, sesame oil, salt, Maui onion, green onions, gochugaru, and toasted macadamia nuts and gently toss with your hands or a wooden spoon. Adjust the seasoning to your liking.

Serve over rice and enjoy immediately.

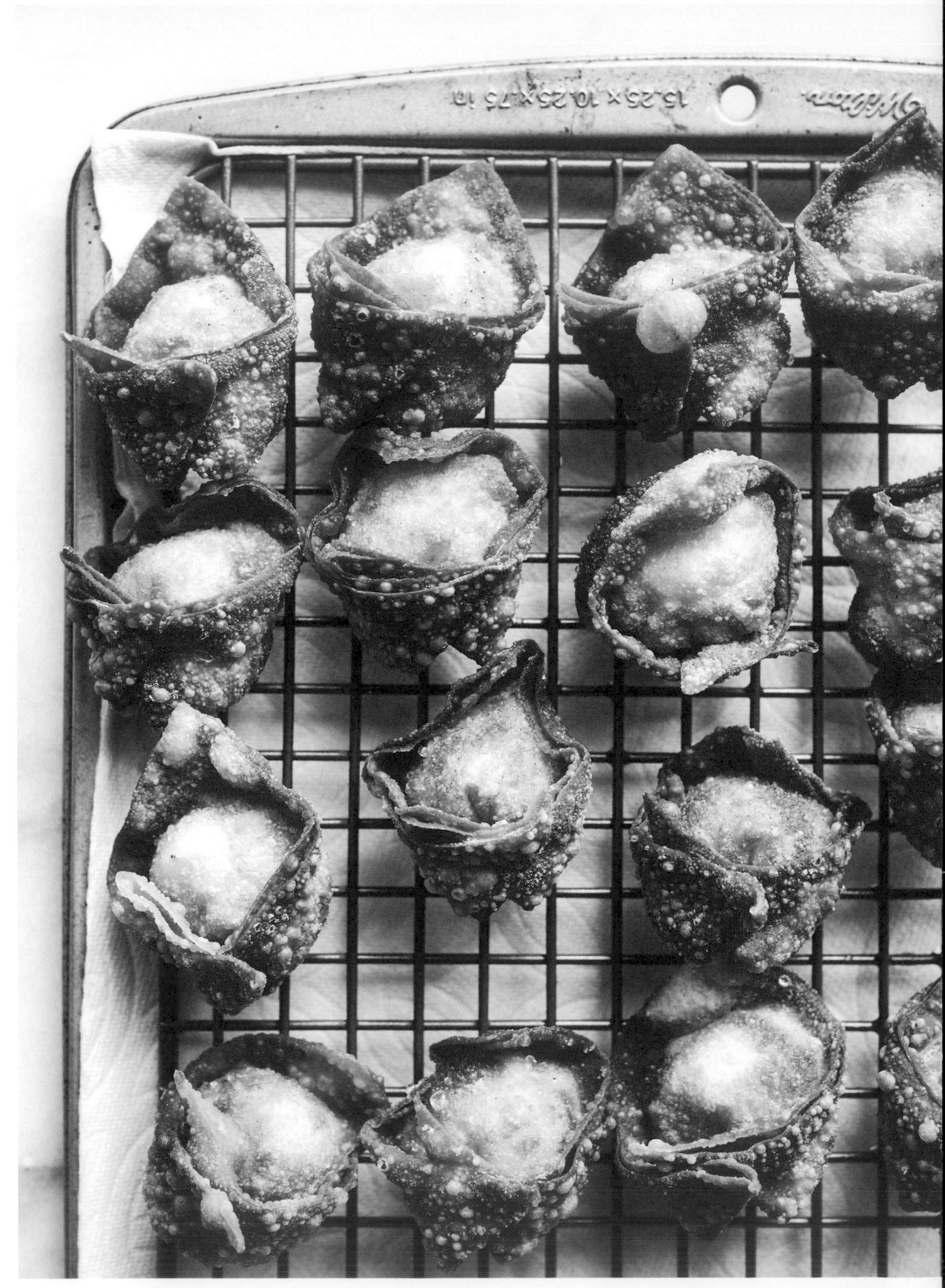
13.25 x 10.25 x .75 in

FRIED WONTONS

4 dried shiitake mushrooms

½ cup hot water

4 ounces medium (41/50) raw shrimp, peeled and deveined, tails removed

12 ounces ground pork

2 garlic cloves, chopped

2 tablespoons oyster sauce

½ teaspoon kosher salt

½ teaspoon freshly ground black pepper, or more to taste

Half 8-ounce can sliced water chestnuts, drained and finely diced

½ cup finely chopped green onions, white and green parts

¼ Maui onion, finely chopped

48 wonton wrappers (pei)

Neutral oil, for deep-frying

Plum sauce, for serving

Chinese hot mustard powder, for serving

Soy sauce (shoyu), for serving

Serves 6 to 8

ON THE MENU:

Namasu, page 68

Maui-Style Kalbi Short Ribs, page 120

Macadamia Nut Cream Pie, page 164

Every memorable hostess has a party trick; this was my mom's. I fondly recall the days when I'd hang out with her in the kitchen, making what at the time felt like millions of wontons. Sometimes called crispy gau gee, these fried dumplings are filled with a deeply flavorful medley of meat and veggies. Growing up, they were snatched off trays at lightning-quick speed, and they'll surely be the hit of your dinner party, too. Uncooked wontons can be frozen, boiled, and added to dishes such as Saimin (page 143) or Oxtail Soup (page 116).

Begin by soaking the shiitake mushrooms in the hot water in a bowl for 10 minutes. Use a smaller bowl to weigh down the mushrooms, if necessary. Finely mince the shrimp with a heavy knife until the shrimp becomes paste-like; alternatively, pulse the shrimp in a food processor until the same paste-like results are achieved. After the shiitake mushrooms have soaked for 10 minutes, drain, press out any excess liquid, and finely dice the mushrooms, discarding the stems. Combine the shiitake, shrimp, pork, garlic, oyster sauce, salt, pepper, water chestnuts, green onions, and Maui onion in a bowl and mix with a wooden spoon until well combined. Do not overmix.

Place a wonton wrapper on a clean, dry surface, arranging it so that points are at the top and the bottom. Place 2 teaspoons of filling in the center of the wonton wrapper. Dip your finger in a small bowl of water and use it to lightly moisten the two top sides of the wrapper. Bring the bottom two sides up to meet the top moistened sides. Press the sides together to seal. If desired, pinch the outer edges from the longer sides of the triangle together. Repeat the process until all the filling and/or wrappers are used.

Line a rimmed baking sheet with paper towels and top with a wire rack. Fill a wide Dutch oven or pot with 2 inches of neutral oil. Warm the oil over medium heat to 350°F. Fry the wontons in small batches until golden brown and cooked through, 4 to 5 minutes. Transfer to the prepared baking sheet to drain. Repeat until all the wontons have been fried.

Serve warm with plum sauce or Chinese hot mustard paste (whisk together equal parts dry mustard powder with cold water until smooth) mixed with soy sauce.

Note: Use the leftover water chestnuts in scrambles, fried rice, or any stir-fry.

MAKI SUSHI

Sushi Rice
4 cups uncooked short-grain rice

⅓ cup rice vinegar

⅓ cup sugar

2 teaspoons kosher salt

Shoyu Tuna
2 teaspoons sugar

2 teaspoons soy sauce (shoyu)

2 teaspoons mirin

One 4-ounce can tuna, in water, drained

Omelet
4 large eggs

1 tablespoon whole milk

Large pinch of kosher salt

1½ teaspoons neutral oil

Quick Pickled Carrots
3 carrots, peeled and julienned

2 tablespoons sugar

2 teaspoons kosher salt

2 tablespoons rice vinegar

1 bunch watercress, ends trimmed

8 sheets roasted sushi nori

One 8½-ounce can seasoned gourd strips with mushroom (makisushi-no-moto), drained (optional)

Makes 6 to 8 rolls

There's a good chance that if you attend a potluck in Maui, at least one family will bring a giant tray of maki sushi from Pukalani Superette. Always a crowd favorite, maki sushi is a sliced, rolled sushi that is stuffed with various seasoned meats and pickled vegetables, ranging from tuna to watercress. The rainbow of fillings looks beautiful and impressive when fanned out on a platter. While making your own maki sushi takes a bit of time, don't let that overwhelm you. Most parts can be made the day before, and you can enlist friends or family to help with the rolling. Call it the pre-party to the actual party!

To make the sushi rice, cook the rice according to the directions of your rice cooker or via stove top if you do not use a rice cooker. While the rice is cooking, in a small saucepan over medium heat, combine the rice vinegar, sugar, and salt and bring to a boil. Cook until the sugar and salt have dissolved. Remove from the heat and let cool slightly while the rice continues to cook. Pour the sauce over the just-cooked rice, tossing, fanning, and fluffing it with a rice paddle. Be careful; the rice is hot. Let the rice cool to room temperature before using.

To make the shoyu tuna, in a small nonstick skillet, combine the sugar, soy sauce, and mirin and bring to a simmer over medium-low heat. Simmer for 1 to 2 minutes, until the sugar dissolves, then add the tuna and cook, stirring often with a wooden spoon, until the liquid evaporates. Remove from the heat and let cool completely before using.

To make the omelet, in a small bowl, whisk together the eggs, milk, and salt until well blended. In a small nonstick skillet, heat 1 teaspoon of the neutral oil over medium-low heat until shiny and shimmering. Pour the egg mixture in and let sit until the edges start to set, about 30 seconds. Push the edges in, toward the center of the pan, with a silicone spatula while tilting the pan to allow the uncooked egg to spread out. Turn the heat to low and cover the pan with a lid. Let sit for 1 to 2 minutes, until almost all the egg has set, then carefully flip the entire omelet over, adding the remaining ½ teaspoon oil to the pan right before you flip. Cook for a minute or so, with the lid off, then remove from the heat and let cool before cutting into ½-inch-wide strips.

To make the quick pickled carrots, prepare an ice-water bath by filling a bowl with a handful of ice cubes and water, and set it aside.

Bring a small pan of water to a simmer over medium heat and quickly blanch the carrots by cooking them in the simmering water for 1 minute, then plunging them into the ice-water bath. Remove the carrots from the bath after a minute or two, reserving the ice-water bath for the watercress. In a small bowl, whisk together the sugar, salt, and rice vinegar and add the carrots. Let sit for 15 minutes; drain the pickling liquid before using.

▶▶▶ Continued

ON THE MENU:

Bring the water in the saucepan back to a simmer over medium heat and blanch the watercress by cooking it in the simmering water until it's wilted, about 30 seconds. Immediately transfer it to the ice bath and let sit until cooled, a minute or two. Drain the watercress and soak up any extra water from the watercress with a couple of paper towels.

Place a sudare (bamboo mat) on a clean work surface, with the bamboo running horizontal. Add a sheet of nori, shiny side facedown, and align the bottom edge with the edge of the sudare. Spread the sushi rice in a thin layer, about ¼ inch thick, leaving a 1½-inch margin on the end farthest from you. Leave a ½-inch margin of rice on the end closest to you and arrange your fillings in a row in this order: omelet, carrots, watercress, seasoned gourd and mushrooms (if using), and tuna, with each row touching the previous row. Carefully roll the sushi away from you, using the mat to apply pressure. Use one hand to keep the filling in place until you get to the point when the mat touches the rice. At this point, lift the mat away from the rice so that you can continue until the sushi is completely rolled. Repeat this process until all the rice has been used.

Cut the rolls into ½-inch-thick slices, fan them out on a platter, and serve.

Note: Use any extra fillings and rice to build a sushi bowl.

MANDOO

Dipping Sauce

2 tablespoons soy sauce
(shoyu)

1 tablespoon rice vinegar

1 tablespoon water

2 teaspoons sugar

¼ teaspoon freshly ground
black pepper

⅛ teaspoon gochugaru
(see page 30)

Mandoo

1 tablespoon plus ½ teaspoon
kosher salt

½ head small napa cabbage
(won bok; about 1 pound),
shredded

12 ounces ground pork

4 ounces medium (41/50) raw
shrimp, peeled and deveined,
tails removed, then chopped

4 green onions, white and
green parts, finely chopped

2 large fresh shiitake
mushrooms, finely diced

One 1-inch piece fresh ginger,
peeled and finely grated

2 garlic cloves, peeled and
finely grated

½ teaspoon freshly ground
black pepper

1 tablespoon sesame oil

One 16-ounce package
mandoo (or gyoza) wrappers
(about 75 wrappers)

Neutral oil, for panfrying

Makes about 75 mandoo

ON THE MENU:

Kim Chee, page 70

Meat Jun, page 123

Liliko'i Chiffon Pie, page 159

Mandoo (mandu) are Korean dumplings. Like their Chinese cousin the wonton, they are usually stuffed with a combination of meat and vegetables. These flavor-filled pockets can be deep-fried, steamed, or, in this case, panfried. They can also be added to soups for nice pops of flavor. There's really very little they can't do. What I love about mandoo is that they can be made in advance, frozen, and then pulled out whenever you're ready for them.

To make the dipping sauce, in a small bowl, whisk together the soy sauce, rice vinegar, water, sugar, black pepper, and gochugaru until the sugar is dissolved. Cover the bowl with plastic wrap and store in the refrigerator until ready to use.

To make the mandoo, in a large bowl, sprinkle 1 tablespoon of the salt over the cabbage. Toss it together with your hands and set aside for 15 minutes to soften. Squeeze out as much moisture as you can from the cabbage (use your hands to do this). In another bowl, combine the cabbage with the pork, shrimp, green onions, mushrooms, ginger, garlic, black pepper, sesame oil, and the remaining ½ teaspoon kosher salt and mix together with your hands or a wooden spoon until combined.

With a wrapper in the palm of your nondominant hand, place a heaping teaspoon of filling in the center of the wrapper. Dip the index finger of your dominant hand in a bowl of warm water and run it along the outer edge of the wrapper. Loosely fold the wrapper in half, into a half-moon shape, and pinch the edge closest to your thumb (in your nondominant hand) closed with your thumb and index finger. Use your dominant hand to fold a series of seven to ten tiny pleats on the front half of the wrapper, pressing each pleat firmly onto the back half of the wrapper. Stand the mandoo on a tray and cover with a clean kitchen towel. Repeat until all the wrappers are used.

Add a few teaspoons of neutral oil to a nonstick skillet and heat over medium heat until shiny and shimmering. Working in batches, place the mandoo upright in the pan, leaving enough room between them so you can turn them all on their sides later. Cook, uncovered, until the bottoms are golden and crispy, 2 to 3 minutes. Turn the mandoo onto their sides (the flatter side), add 2 to 3 tablespoons water, and immediately (and carefully) cover the pan with a lid to steam them. Cook until the bottoms are crispy and the dumplings are cooked through, 3 to 4 minutes. Repeat until all the dumplings are cooked. Serve hot with the dipping sauce.

Note: Alternatively, you can freeze any dumplings you are not planning to serve immediately. Place the uncooked dumplings onto a baking sheet, and slip into the freezer for 30 minutes, then transfer them to a ziplock freezer bag. To cook frozen dumplings, follow the same directions, adding a couple of extra minutes to the steaming time.

LUMPIA

1 tablespoon neutral oil, plus more for frying

½ Maui or yellow onion, finely diced

2 pounds ground pork

1 teaspoon kosher salt

1 teaspoon freshly ground black pepper

4 garlic cloves, peeled and finely minced

4 carrots, peeled and julienned

6 to 8 green onions, green parts only, chopped

4 ounces bean thread noodles (see page 28), soaked in hot water for 30 minutes, drained, and cut in half

2 tablespoons soy sauce (shoyu)

2 teaspoons fish sauce

1 teaspoon sesame oil

One 16-ounce package Chinese spring roll (lumpia) wrappers (about 30 wrappers)

Sweet chili sauce, for dipping (Mae Ploy brand preferred)

Serves 6 to 8

ON THE MENU:

Mac Salad, page 55

Pork and Peas, page 94

Sweet Potato Haupia Bars, page 171

The first time I ever had lumpia was at the Maui County fair. I still remember it as the best I've ever had—the crispy, thin wrapper shattered the second I bit into it, and the filling was so flavorful. If you ever happen to be in Maui at the beginning of October, I highly recommend you check out the fair, and wear your stretchy pants! While it's easy to assume lumpia is Chinese because it looks a lot like an egg roll, it's actually Filipino. However, it was introduced to the Philippines by Chinese immigrants, so there is a reason the two are so similar. As similar as they are, there is one main difference. Lumpia skins are paper-thin, while egg roll wrappers are usually denser, like wontons. Look for them in the freezer section at an Asian market. Fun fact: Not all lumpia are savory. Banana lumpia are also very popular in Hawai'i and usually made with small, tart apple bananas.

In a large skillet, heat 1 tablespoon neutral oil over medium heat until shiny and shimmering. Add the Maui onion and sauté until almost translucent, 4 to 5 minutes. Add the pork and sauté until the meat is browned, about 3 minutes, breaking up the meat with a wooden spoon as it browns. Season the mixture with the salt and pepper, add the garlic, and cook for a minute or two. Add the carrots and cook until they are tender, about 3 minutes. Add the green onions, bean thread noodles, soy sauce, fish sauce, and sesame oil and sauté for a minute or two more. Remove from the heat and let cool completely before using.

While the filling is cooling, peel apart all the wrappers. Start by placing the stack of wrappers under a damp, clean kitchen towel, with another damp towel ready nearby. Peel off one wrapper, place the shiny side down, and cover with the other damp kitchen towel. Repeat until all the wrappers are peeled apart and loosely stacked under the towel.

Place a wrapper, shiny side down, so that the two corners are pointing away from and toward you. Place 3 tablespoons filling near the corner edge closest to you, arranging the filling so that it forms a line perpendicular to the top and bottom corners. Roll the edge of the wrapper toward the middle, away from you, rolling until you reach about the halfway point. Fold both sides in, keeping everything as tight as possible, and continue rolling. Dip your finger in a small bowl of water and run it along the outer edge of the wrapper to seal it. Repeat until all the filling and/or wrappers are used.

Line a large platter with paper towels and heat 1 inch of neutral oil in a large skillet over medium-low heat until it is shiny and hot. Fry the rolls in batches until golden and crispy, 2 to 3 minutes on each side. Set on the prepared plate to drain. Serve warm with the sweet chili sauce.

CONE SUSHI

Cone Sushi Rice

3 cups uncooked short-grain rice

1 carrot, peeled, julienned, and chopped into ½-inch lengths

⅓ cup plus 3 tablespoons rice vinegar

½ cup sugar

2½ teaspoons kosher salt

Seasoned Aburage

9 fried bean curds (aburage), cut in half on the diagonal

1 teaspoon dashi granules

1½ cups water

3 tablespoons sugar

2 tablespoons mirin

2 tablespoons sake

3 tablespoons soy sauce (shoyu)

Makes 18 cone sushi

ON THE MENU:

Pohole Fern Salad, page 62
Mochiko Chicken, page 100
Pie Crust Manju, page 179

Also called inari, cone sushi gets its name from its conical shape. Squares of seasoned aburage (fried bean curd) are cut in half to form cones, and sushi rice is stuffed inside. Miyako Sushi, Inc., in Wailuku on the island of Maui, makes my favorite cone sushi. It is perfectly balanced: not too sweet, not too salty, and never greasy. To find aburage, check the freezer section of an Asian market, or look for a place that makes tofu, as chances are they make aburage too. Dashi (broth) granules can be found in the Asian section of most supermarkets.

To make the cone sushi rice, cook the rice according to the directions of your rice cooker or via stove top if you do not use a rice cooker. While the rice is cooking, fill a small saucepan halfway with water and bring to a simmer. Add the carrot and cook until the carrot is tender, a minute or two. Drain the water from the pan and transfer the carrot to a small bowl. Return the small saucepan to the stove top; add the vinegar, sugar, and salt; and bring to a boil over medium heat. Cook for 2 to 3 minutes, until the sugar and salt have dissolved. Remove from the heat and let cool slightly while the rice continues to cook. Combine the just-cooked rice with the carrot and pour the sauce over the rice, tossing, fanning, and fluffing it with a rice paddle. Be careful; the rice is hot.

To make the seasoned aburage, bring a large saucepan filled halfway with water to a boil over high heat. Turn the heat to medium, then add the bean curds and cook for 2 minutes; this helps to remove the oil from the curds. Drain the water from the pan and transfer the bean curds to a plate. In the same saucepan, combine the dashi granules, water, sugar, mirin, sake, and soy sauce and bring to a boil over high heat. Add the bean curds and turn the heat to medium-low. Simmer for 15 minutes, then remove from the heat and let cool to room temperature in the pan.

Once cool, drain the sauce from the pan and gently press or squeeze any remaining liquid from the aburage. Separate the tofu insides from the outer fried skin, or wrapper, of the aburage. Mix the inside tofu bits into the seasoned sushi rice. Fill the aburage pouches with the rice, pressing gently to pack lightly, and serve at room temperature.

SIDES

Don't be fooled by the word "side": in Hawaiʻi, most meals are accompanied by at least one side dish. They're essential when building a proper plate lunch (see page 20): Kālua Pig (page 83) is almost always paired with Lomi Salmon (page 59) and Poi (page 65), and in my house, Takuan (page 69) and Mochiko Chicken (page 100) are always served together! From pickles to mayo-y salads, here are a few of the many sides you will find in the islands.

MAC SALAD

8 ounces dry elbow macaroni

Kosher salt

2 tablespoons grated Maui or yellow onion (roughly ¼ whole onion)

1 to 1½ cups Best Foods (or Hellmann's) mayonnaise

2 tablespoons sweet pickle juice

3 tablespoons sweet pickle relish

Freshly ground black pepper

¼ cup coarsely grated carrot (½ medium carrot)

Serves 6 to 8

ON THE MENU:

Takuan, page 69

Local-Style BBQ Chicken, page 108

Butter Mochi, page 167

"I'm obsessed with Hawaiian mac salad!" I can't tell you how many friends from the mainland have said this very sentence to me. It's usually followed by "What's the secret ingredient?" Well, I think the answer is grated onions. Yes, pull out your box grater and grate your onions with the small grate side, making sure to add all the liquid goodness that weeps out. You want your onions to be almost liquefied to get that Hawai'i-style mac salad flavor. This salad is served with almost every plate lunch and at most family gatherings. There are many variations— with green onions, peas, chopped ham, or even tuna—but this recipe makes a good basic island-style mac salad. And because it's my favorite, I've also included a variation with potato and hard-boiled eggs.

Cook the macaroni, salting the water with 2 tablespoons kosher salt, according to the instructions on the package, until very tender, not al dente. Drain and transfer to a large bowl. Let cool slightly for 10 minutes, then add the onion, ½ cup of the mayonnaise, the pickle juice, relish, and pepper to taste and toss until well coated. Taste and season as needed with salt and pepper. Chill for 1 hour.

When ready to serve, stir in ½ cup of the mayonnaise and the carrot; add more mayonnaise if it looks dry. Taste and adjust the seasoning as needed. Serve chilled.

POTATO MAC SALAD

Kosher salt

3 medium russet potatoes, peeled and cut into 1-inch cubes

8 ounces dry elbow macaroni

4 large hard-boiled eggs, peeled and coarsely chopped

3 tablespoons grated Maui or yellow onion (roughly ⅓ whole onion)

1½ to 2 cups Best Foods (or Hellmann's) mayonnaise

3 tablespoons sweet pickle juice

¼ cup sweet pickle relish

Freshly ground black pepper

¼ cup coarsely grated carrot (½ medium carrot)

Bring a large pot of water to a boil over high heat, then add 2 tablespoons kosher salt and the cubed potatoes. Turn the heat to medium-high and cook until fork-tender, 10 to 12 minutes. Drain and transfer to a large bowl.

Meanwhile, cook the macaroni, salting the water with 2 tablespoons kosher salt, according to the instructions on the package, until very tender, not al dente. Drain and add to the bowl with the potatoes. Let cool slightly for 10 minutes, then add the eggs, onion, 1 cup of the mayonnaise, the pickle juice, relish, and pepper to taste and toss until well coated. Taste and season as needed with salt and pepper. Chill for 1 hour.

When ready to serve, stir in ½ cup of the mayonnaise and the carrot; add more mayonnaise if it looks dry. Taste and adjust the seasoning as needed. Serve chilled.

CHICKEN LONG RICE

1½ pounds skin-on, bone-in chicken thighs

12 cups chicken broth

5 garlic cloves, peeled and lightly smashed

One 5-inch piece fresh ginger, peeled and thinly julienned

1½ teaspoons Hawaiian salt ('alaea)

One 5.3-ounce package bean thread noodles (see page 28)

6 green onions, white and green parts, chopped

Serves 6 to 8

ON THE MENU:

Poi, page 65

Pork Laulau, page 78

Haupia, page 168

Chicken long rice is often assumed to be a Hawaiian dish, as it's served at most lūʻau with poi, lomi salmon, laulau, and kālua pig, but it actually originated as a Chinese noodle dish. And while it's commonly served as a side dish at lūʻau, it can stand alone as a rainy-day soup. If you're serving it as a main dish, I recommend adding some veggies, like carrots, sweet onions, and mushrooms.

Place the chicken, broth, garlic, three-quarters of the ginger, and the salt into a large pot. Bring everything to a boil over high heat, then turn the heat to medium-low and simmer with the lid on until the chicken is tender, about 45 minutes. Skim off the surface of the broth periodically while simmering. Once the chicken is cooked, remove it from the broth and place on a plate to cool slightly. Continue simmering the broth while the chicken cools.

Meanwhile, place the bean thread noodles in a large bowl and cover with cold water. Let sit for 30 minutes to hydrate and soften the noodles; drain the water from the bowl and cut the soaked noodles in half or thirds with a pair of kitchen shears.

When the chicken is cool enough to touch, remove the skin and bones and cut the meat into bite-size pieces. Add the meat back to the broth, along with half of the green onions, and continue to simmer. Skim any scum that may form. Add the hydrated bean thread noodles to the broth and simmer for another 10 minutes, until the noodles are clear, plumped, and tender. Garnish with the remaining julienned ginger and chopped green onions and serve hot.

LOMI
SALMON

½ pound salmon fillet, skinned and boned

¼ cup Hawaiian salt ('alaea)

4 Roma tomatoes, seeded and chopped

2 small Maui onions, peeled and chopped

6 green onions, green parts only, chopped

¼ teaspoon gochugaru (see page 30)

Serves 6 to 8

ON THE MENU:

Poi, page 65

Kālua Pig, page 83

Sweet Potato Haupia Bars, page 171

A vestige of the whaling industry, lomi salmon is a staple at lū'au and grocery stores alike. While it's common to find salt (salted) salmon and lomi salmon in grocery stores in Hawai'i, I have learned that is not the case on the mainland and the rest of the world. That makes this recipe a two-day affair, as the salmon takes a day to cure in the salt. Better ingredients make for a better lomi salmon, so look for fresh salmon, ripe tomatoes, and sweet onions.

Place the salmon in a nonreactive rimmed dish or pan large enough for the fillet to lie flat and evenly coat both sides with the salt. Cover the dish with plastic wrap and refrigerate for 24 hours.

The next day, prepare an ice-water bath by filling a large bowl with a handful of ice and water.

Rinse the salt from the fish and soak the fish in the ice-water bath for 1 hour. Slice the salmon into ¼- to ½-inch cubes and place them into a nonreactive bowl. Add the tomatoes, Maui onions, green onions, and gochugaru and gently toss with your hands. Cover the bowl with plastic wrap and refrigerate for several hours before serving.

POHOLE FERN SALAD

1 pound pohole fern

1 pound cherry tomatoes, quartered

½ small Maui onion, thinly sliced lengthwise

5 green onions, green parts only, chopped

1 tablespoon fish sauce

¼ cup soy sauce (shoyu)

3 tablespoons rice vinegar

2 tablespoons sesame oil

¼ cup sugar

Serves 6 to 8

ON THE MENU:

Poi, page 65

Chinese-Style Steamed Fish, page 133

Kūlolo Bars, page 176

If I were writing a book about pohole fern, I would call it *Pohole: A Fern of Many Names*. It is called ostrich fern on the mainland, pohole fern on Maui, hōʻiʻo on Oʻahu, pako in the Philippines, warabi in Japan, and kosade in Korea. A foraged fern shoot, pohole are bright green, unfurled fern heads that are harvested when they're young and anywhere from 6 to 9 inches in height. The distinctive flavor can be described as nutty and mildly sweet, and the texture is akin to okra on the inside and young asparagus on the outside. Before using, snap off the ends of the fern shoot, the same way you would for asparagus. Paired with a sweet umami sauce and bright cherry tomatoes, this salad is a crowd-pleaser.

Prepare an ice-water bath by filling a large bowl with a handful of ice cubes and water, and set it aside. Wash and remove any little "hairs" from the pohole fern shoots. Cut the shoots into 1½-inch segments and blanch for 1 minute in a pot of boiling water. Drain the shoots into a colander and immediately transfer them to the ice-water bath. Once cooled, drain the water from the ferns and place them in a bowl with the tomatoes, Maui onions, and green onions.

In a small bowl, whisk together the fish sauce, soy sauce, vinegar, oil, and sugar until the sugar has dissolved. Pour the mixture over the vegetables and gently toss with your hands. Cover the bowl with plastic wrap and refrigerate for several hours before serving.

Note: Fresh pohole will keep in the refrigerator for about a week. If you aren't in Hawaiʻi, I'd recommend checking with a specialty foods purveyor to help you source the fern.

POI

2 pounds taro (kalo) root, cleaned

½ to ⅔ cup water

Serves 4 to 6

ON THE MENU:

Lomi Salmon, page 59
Fried Reef Fish, page 136
Haupia, page 168

Nowadays you can find fresh poi in grocery stores all over the islands. It's made commercially by companies such as Hanalei Poi on Kaua'i and Taro Brand on O'ahu. However, before it was made in bulk with modern machinery, steamed and peeled taro (kalo) root was pounded by hand on beautiful papa ku'i 'ai (wooden boards) using pōhaku ku'i 'ai (stone pestles). This created a thick substance called pa'i 'ai; by adding water to it, you create poi. While the OG (original gangsta) process is very satisfying, I understand if you don't have access to a board and pestle. To make poi at home, you'll need a high-speed food processor. To find taro root, take a trip to an Asian market and ask someone to help you find a medium-size taro, gabi, dasheen, or malanga corm that weighs around 2 pounds.

Bring a large pot of water to boil over high heat. Add the taro, turn the heat to medium-low, and cook until very tender, about 1 hour. You can test this by inserting a fork into the taro; if it's very easy to pierce the taro, it's done. Drain off the water and let the taro rest until it is cool enough to pick up.

Wearing disposable gloves and using the side of a spoon, peel the skin off the taro. Be sure to remove all the skin.

Transfer the cooked and peeled taro to your food processor with ½ cup of the water. Process on high speed for 3 minutes, then scrape down the sides. Process until smooth, about 2 minutes more. You can add more water if necessary—the final consistency should be thick and smooth like molasses.

You can serve the poi immediately or allow it to age a day or two. If you are aging your poi, carefully pour a layer of water over it to prevent a skin from forming on the top. Simply pour off the water when you are ready to serve it. The poi will keep for 3 days stored in an airtight container in the refrigerator.

Note: Be sure to wear disposable gloves when handling raw taro, as the calcium oxalate crystals in its skin and leaves are irritating and can cause a rash. This is also why taro cannot be consumed in its raw form; it must be cooked.

PICKLED ONION

4 Maui or yellow onions

1 cup distilled white vinegar

1 cup water

1½ tablespoons Hawaiian salt ('alaea)

¾ cup sugar

2 Hawaiian chili peppers (nīoi), finely diced

Makes about 1 quart

ON THE MENU:

Mac Salad, page 55

Beef Stew, page 127

Malasadas, page 183

Sabula de vinha, or pickled onion, is a great way to add crunch, tang, and a little flavor to any dish. It can be sweet or hot and, like kim chee, is found in local grocery stores across the state. I prefer my pickled onions sweet, but if you are not a fan of sweet pickled onions or are trying to minimize your sugar intake, feel free to cut back on the sugar listed here.

Cut the onions in half lengthwise, from the bulb end to the top of the onion, and remove the papery outer skins. Cut off any dried root ends without cutting off the entire bottom of the onion. This is important because you want to keep the wedges intact, if possible. From there, simply cut the halves into ½-inch wedges and layer and pack them into a quart-size jar.

In a small, nonreactive saucepan, combine the vinegar, water, salt, sugar, and chili peppers and bring to a boil over medium-high heat. As soon as the mixture comes to a boil, remove the pan from the heat and let cool for 5 minutes. Pour the hot mixture over the onions and cover the jar. Let cool to room temperature before transferring the jar to the refrigerator. Chill for 2 days before serving. This will keep for two weeks in the refrigerator.

NAMASU

¾ cup plus 1 tablespoon rice vinegar

¾ cup sugar

2 Japanese cucumbers, or 1 English cucumber, sliced into ¼-inch-thick rounds

1 medium carrot, peeled and julienned

½ daikon radish (about 1¼ pounds), peeled and julienned

2 teaspoons Hawaiian salt ('alaea)

Makes about 1 quart

ON THE MENU:

Potato Mac Salad, page 55
Chicken Katsu, page 111
Cascaron, page 180

When you look at most meals in Hawai'i, you'll usually see a main, a starch (probably rice), and a bunch of sides. We're talking Kim Chee (page 70), Mac Salad (page 55), Lomi Salmon (page 59), or something pickled. Namasu is a Japanese-style vinegar-dressed dish. It's typically made with cucumbers, though it's not uncommon to find it with carrots and daikon, as well as limu (ogo), bean sprouts, lotus root, or even celery. And the options aren't just limited to plants. There are many recipes that add clam, crab, abalone, and shrimp (both dried and freshly cooked). My mom always has some version of this side on hand, and she pulls it out for pretty much every meal—breakfast included.

In a nonreactive saucepan over medium heat, stir the vinegar and sugar together and cook until the sugar has dissolved. Remove from the heat and let cool to room temperature.

In a mixing bowl, toss the cucumbers, carrot, and daikon with the salt. Let sit for 30 minutes. Rinse and drain thoroughly. Place the vegetables in a jar and cover with the vinegar mixture. Cover and chill in the refrigerator for 24 hours before serving. This will keep for 2 weeks in the refrigerator.

TAKUAN

1 large or 2 small firm daikon radishes (about 2½ pounds), peeled

¼ cup Hawaiian salt ('alaea)

½ cup rice vinegar

1½ cups sugar

3 or 4 squeezes of yellow food coloring gel (optional)

1 Hawaiian chili pepper (nīoi), thinly sliced (optional)

Makes about 1 quart

ON THE MENU:

Cone Sushi, page 51

Chicken Katsu, page 111

Gau, page 186

Growing up, I never stopped to question what the bright yellow–colored pickled veggies sitting next to my rice were. My mom used to pull a giant jar out of the fridge most mornings to serve with our eggs and rice. I'd find them in my bentos for lunch, and they were almost always found on the dinner table. The scent is a bit of a surprise, but the combination of pungent daikon (a long white radish), tangy vinegar, and sweet-and-salty crunch more than makes up for the shock. The trick to this pickle is a bit of patience. You'll need to let them sit for at least 3 days before serving. Crunchy and a little funky smelling (in the best way), this pickled daikon is the perfect accompaniment to just about any savory dish, but my favorites are Mochiko Chicken (page 100) or Teriyaki Beef Sticks (page 119) and rice. Be sure to look for a firm daikon radish, as you'll need it for the crunch!

Cut the daikon into ⅜-inch-thick rounds and toss with the salt. Let sit uncovered at room temperature for 3 hours, then rinse and squeeze out the excess water before packing it into a jar. Meanwhile, combine the vinegar, sugar, food coloring, and chili pepper (if using) in a small, nonreactive saucepan and bring to a boil. Cool the sugar-vinegar sauce to room temperature while the daikon sits. Pour it over the prepared daikon slices in the jar and store in the refrigerator for at least 3 days but preferably a week before serving. This will keep for 2 weeks in the refrigerator.

KIM CHEE

One 3-pound head napa
cabbage (won bok)

¾ cup Hawaiian salt ('alaea)

1½ tablespoons gochugaru
(see page 30)

One 3-inch piece fresh ginger,
peeled and finely grated
(about 1½ teaspoons)

4 or 5 garlic cloves, peeled
and finely grated (about
1½ teaspoons)

1 teaspoon sugar

5 green onions, white and
green parts, chopped into
1½-inch pieces (optional)

Makes about 1 quart

ON THE MENU:

Mandoo, page 47

Meat Jun, page 123

Shave Ice, page 172

Hot and spicy, this Korean pickle, commonly spelled kimchi, is a staple in most Hawai'i fridges. From Halm's to Kohala, you can find a variety of kim chee on grocery-store shelves. NOH Foods even sells a kim chee seasoning packet. And while it's typically made with napa cabbage (won bok), you can also find varieties made with cucumber, daikon, and limu (ogo). Kim chee is great with dishes like Maui-Style Kalbi Short Ribs (page 120), Shoyu Chicken (page 103), and even eggs and rice in the morning! You can also chop it up and add it to your fried rice.

Cut off the tough ends and core the cabbage, then cut it into 1½-inch pieces. Rinse the cabbage in cold water and drain in a colander before placing the pieces into a large bowl. Sprinkle the salt all over the cabbage and gently massage it in. Let the cabbage sit for a total of 4 hours, massaging it every 30 minutes. Rinse the cabbage thoroughly in cold water, repeat, then drain in a colander.

Clean the cabbage bowl and add the gochugaru, ginger, garlic, and sugar. Put on a pair of disposable gloves and work in the ingredients with your hands until thoroughly combined; it should form a cohesive paste. Return the cabbage to the bowl along with the green onions (if using) and mix everything well with your hands. Be sure to evenly coat the cabbage pieces in the paste. Alternatively, you can mix the paste together with a wooden spoon before mixing the cabbage in.

Transfer the mixture to a quart-size jar, packing the cabbage tightly, and cover it with a piece of plastic wrap followed by a tight-fitting lid. Store in a cool, dark, dry spot for 2 days to ferment slightly. Open the lid twice daily, once in the morning and once at night, to let any gases out and to prevent the jar from exploding.

After 2 days, transfer the jar to the refrigerator to slowly ferment for another 3 days before serving. This will keep, refrigerated, for about a month.

PORTUGUESE SAUSAGE PATTIES

1 pound well-marbled
ground pork

4 garlic cloves, peeled and
finely grated

1 or 2 Hawaiian chili peppers
(nīoi), finely minced

½ teaspoon Portuguese Spice
Blend (recipe follows)

1 tablespoon paprika

½ tablespoon kosher salt

1 teaspoon freshly ground
black pepper

2 tablespoons red wine
vinegar

Neutral oil, for frying

Serves 4 to 6

ON THE MENU:

Cornbread, page 74

Beef Chili, page 128

Ice Cake, page 175

Linguiça, more commonly referred to as Portuguese sausage, is one of my favorite tastes of home. When I was in college, I'd freeze a bunch of Hawaiian Sausage Company Portuguese Brand Sausage (Hot), wrap them up in foil, and bring them back to San Diego with me. Nowadays, I pick them up in my local Marukai Market in Los Angeles, but on days when I don't feel like making a special trip to Little Tokyo, I make my own, in patty form. Packed with spice and garlic, Portuguese sausage is the perfect addition to your breakfast plate. I serve it with my soft scrambled eggs and steamed white rice. This combination is so popular that you can even find a Portuguese sausage breakfast plate at the local McDonald's in Hawai'i. But please don't think this side is limited to breakfast; you can also use it in recipes such as Beef Chili (page 128), Portuguese Bean Soup (page 97), and Local-Style Fish (page 137).

In large bowl, combine the pork, garlic, chili pepper, spice blend, paprika, salt, pepper, and vinegar and mix with a wooden spoon or heavy spatula until well combined. Cover the bowl with plastic wrap and refrigerate for 24 hours to allow the flavors to meld and mellow.

The next day, scoop up about 2 tablespoons of meat and shape it into a ball. Flatten the ball with the palms of your hands to form a small, ¼-inch-thick patty. Repeat this process until all the meat has been formed. Be sure to place a piece of parchment between the patties if you are layering them. (The patties can be stored in the refrigerator in a covered container for 3 to 4 days or frozen for up to 1 month.)

Warm a tablespoon or two of oil in a skillet over medium heat and place as many patties as can fit without touching in the pan. Cook for 3 to 4 minutes on each side, until evenly browned and cooked through. Serve immediately.

PORTUGUESE SPICE BLEND

Two 3-inch sticks cinnamon, broken
into pieces with a heavy knife

1 teaspoon whole cloves

2 tablespoons whole black
peppercorns

1 whole star anise

1 bay leaf

Makes about ¼ cup

Preheat the oven to 300°F. On a small rimmed baking sheet, evenly spread out the cinnamon, cloves, peppercorns, anise, and bay leaf. Toast in the oven until the bay leaf is golden brown and the spices are very aromatic, 15 to 20 minutes. Let the spices and bay leaf cool on the pan for at least 5 minutes, or until cool enough to touch, before transferring them to a spice or coffee grinder. Grind until all the spices are finely ground, about a minute or two. Transfer to a small airtight container and store for up to 2 months.

CORNBREAD

½ cup cornmeal

1½ cups all-purpose flour

½ cup sugar

1 teaspoon baking soda

1 teaspoon baking powder

½ teaspoon kosher salt

¼ cup neutral oil

¼ cup unsalted butter, melted

2 large eggs, lightly beaten

1 teaspoon vanilla extract

1 tablespoon honey

1¼ cups buttermilk, shaken

Makes one 8-inch square or
round pan

ON THE MENU:

Lumpia, page 48

Portuguese Bean Soup,
page 97

Double-Chocolate Haupia Pie,
page 163

I'm a huge fan of cornbread because it comes together with very little work and adds a bit of sweetness to savory, hearty dishes such as Beef Stew (page 127), Portuguese Bean Soup (page 97), or even Beef Chili (page 128). While it may seem out of place in a cookbook all about local Hawai'i eats, it's actually quite common. It's possible it came to our tables in the form of the dense, savory Portuguese broa (or cornbread); nowadays it's most frequently enjoyed as a light, sweet corn cake. Substitute it for the steamed white rice you typically serve with your hearty soups and stews or, if you prefer, in addition to that starchy staple.

Preheat the oven to 350°F. Grease an 8-inch square or round baking pan.

In a large bowl, whisk together the cornmeal, flour, sugar, baking soda, baking powder, and salt. Whisk in the oil, melted butter, eggs, vanilla, honey, and buttermilk. Stir until everything is well combined.

Pour the mixture into the prepared pan and bake until golden brown and a toothpick inserted into the center of the pan comes out clean, 35 to 40 minutes. Let cool on a baking rack for 10 minutes before cutting into 8 to 10 squares or wedges. Serve warm.

PORK

(Pua'a)

It's easy to see that Hawai'i has an affinity for pork. Whether it is steamed and baked in an imu (an earthen oven), stewed, or comes in a can and is panfried, we find many ways to prepare this protein. Try packing up some Soy-Glazed Spam Musubi (page 90) for a picnic or making a batch of Portuguese Bean Soup (page 97) for your next family potluck.

PORK LAULAU

12 ounces North Pacific sablefish (butterfish), cut into 8 equal pieces

Hawaiian salt ('alaea)

24 taro (kalo or lū'au) leaves (see Note, page 80) or Swiss chard leaves

16 ti leaves

2 pounds pork butt, with a fat cap, cut into 8 pieces

Serves 6 to 8

ON THE MENU:

Lomi Salmon, page 59

Chicken Long Rice, page 56

Sweet Potato Haupia Bars, page 171

A traditional Hawaiian dish, laulau consists of a protein, like pork, beef, or chicken and salted butterfish, wrapped in lū'au (taro or kalo) leaves, then ti leaves, and steamed. It was traditionally cooked in an imu (earthen oven), but today it is more commonly steamed on the stove top in a steamer basket or a pressure cooker. If you don't have access to lū'au leaves, Swiss chard makes an excellent substitute. If you can't find ti leaves, 'a'ole pilikia (no problem)—use 10-inch squares of parchment paper instead!

Sprinkle each piece of sablefish with a pinch of salt and set aside.

Wearing disposable gloves (see Note, page 65), wash the taro leaves and use a paring knife to remove the center stem and any tough veins. If using chard, do the same, and also blanch the leaves until softened. Wash and prepare the ti leaves by stripping off the stiff rib in the middle of the leaf by cutting a small notch about midway down the leaf and gently removing it while leaving the leaf intact.

▶▶▶ Continued

▶▶▶ Pork Laulau, Continued

Assemble the parcels (see page 79 for step-by-step photographs) by stacking 3 taro leaves, vein side down, with the largest leaf on the bottom, then place a piece of pork and a piece of salted sablefish in the middle. Fold the left and right sides in, then fold the bottom up before folding the top over and rolling it until the parcel is closed. Repeat this until all the leaves and meat are used. Place 2 ti leaves down, forming a cross. Place a taro leaf parcel in the middle, fold the first leaf over the bundle, and continue to fold until the parcel is contained, then wrap the other ti leaf around it in the opposite direction. If using parchment squares, fold the left and right sides in before folding up the bottom and then folding down the top. Secure the bundles with kitchen string.

Fill a large pot with 2 inches of water, cover, and bring to a boil over high heat. Place a steamer basket in the pot and turn the heat to low. Place the laulau in the steamer basket and replace the lid. Steam, replenishing the water as needed, for 4 hours to cook off the calcium oxalate in the taro leaves; if you're using Swiss chard, steam for 3 hours. Alternatively, you can steam in a pressure cooker at full pressure for 45 minutes. Serve warm, unwrapping and discarding the ti leaves before eating.

Note: You must cook the taro leaves completely to remove the calcium oxalate. If you don't, your mouth and throat will be a little itchy.

KĀLUA PIG

One 5½-pound boneless
pork butt, with fat cap

1 tablespoon neutral oil

3 tablespoons Hawaiian salt
('alaea), plus more as needed

2 frozen banana leaves,
thawed, or 4 large ti leaves,
tough stems removed

2 teaspoons liquid smoke
(see page 30)

Serves 6 to 8

ON THE MENU:

Pohole Fern Salad, page 62
Lomi Salmon, page 59
Haupia, page 168

If you're ever given an opportunity to experience making a traditional imu, or earthen oven, I would highly recommend it. It is incredible to see how the imu goes from a freshly dug pit, lined with kindling, dried kiawe wood, and porous lava rocks, to what looks like a pit of burning lava, the formerly black rocks now transformed into bright red balls of fire. It's a remarkable sight, but it's that magical moment when the moist banana stumps are laid down and the air is filled with smoke, steam, and sugar that gives me chicken skin (aka goosebumps). All of this needs to happen before the pig and various other items, like laulau and 'ulu (breadfruit), can go in, get covered with banana leaves and/or ti leaves, moist burlap sacks and tarps, and finally a layer of earth. After that, it's a waiting game, as the imu does its job, steaming and smoking the food for 6 to 8 hours. The unearthing feels well earned and is greatly anticipated, the aroma intoxicating.

While I can't give you quite the same experience at home, I have devised the next best thing. In your roasting pan, you will create your own mini imu, where you can steam and smoke your pig all in the comfort of your own kitchen. A note about the banana leaves: It's essential to use previously frozen ones. The fresh leaves are not as malleable as frozen varieties and end up tearing too easily when wrapped around the pork. Look for them in an Asian market.

Leftovers are great sandwiched between Sweet Bread Rolls (page 191).

Preheat the oven to 325°F. Set a rack in a roasting pan. Using a small, sharp knife, cut 1-inch slits all over the pork. Coat the entire surface of the pork with the oil before rubbing it with the salt. Place 1 banana leaf on a clean work surface and set the pork in the middle of the leaf. Wrap the leaf around the pork, completely enveloping it in the leaf. Repeat, this time placing the leaf on the top, covering the ends of the first leaf, and wrapping it around to the bottom. If you're using ti leaves, repeat two more times until the pork butt is completely wrapped. Secure the leaves on all four sides with a long piece of kitchen string, as if you're tying up a box. Pour water into a roasting pan until it reaches just below the roasting rack; make sure you've got at least ½ inch of water. Add the liquid smoke. Place the roast on the rack and cover the entire pan with aluminum foil.

Roast until the pork roast is very tender, about 6 hours. You can test this by poking it with a fork; if the fork is easily inserted, it's ready. Transfer the wrapped pork to a rack set on a rimmed baking sheet and let sit for 10 to 20 minutes. Unwrap the pork and use two forks to pull or shred the meat. Taste the pork and sprinkle it with more salt, if necessary. If the meat is dry, add boiling water directly to the shredded pork to moisten as necessary. Serve immediately.

CHAR SIU PORK

4 pounds pork butt, cut into 1½-inch-wide strips

1 tablespoon Hawaiian salt ('alaea)

1 cup packed brown sugar

⅓ cup mild honey

1½ teaspoons Chinese five-spice powder

¼ cup hoisin sauce

3 tablespoons whiskey

¾ teaspoon red gel food coloring, or 1½ teaspoons red liquid food coloring (optional)

Serves 6 to 8; recipe can be halved

ON THE MENU:

Fried Wontons, page 41

Kim Chee, page 70

Gau, page 186

If you take a walk through Chinatown on O'ahu, you might be drawn to the rainbow of exotic produce, expertly stacked in perfect lines, or the row of lei and flower shops, but I find myself gravitating toward the windows filled with glistening roast duck and shiny red char siu (Chinese roast pork). The smell is intoxicating; it's hard not to let your nose lead you there. While absolutely capable of standing alone as a meal, you will often find char siu stuffed in buns (Manapua, page 197), topping noodle dishes like Saimin (page 143) and Somen Salad (page 151), or added to fried rice. If you've built up your Hawai'i pantry (see "Building Your Pantry," page 27), you should have everything you need, with exception of one key ingredient: hoisin. Hoisin is a thick, dark sauce that's packed with a range of flavors such as ginger, cinnamon, garlic, soy, and sesame. It's delicious. My favorite brand is Lee Kum Kee, and you can find it the Asian foods section of most grocery stores. A note about the char siu's red color: While it's typical, it's not necessary and doesn't add anything but that—color.

Rub the pork butt strips with the salt and place in a wide rimmed pan or in a gallon-size ziplock bag. In a small bowl, combine the brown sugar, honey, five-spice powder, hoisin, whiskey, and red food coloring (if using) to make a marinade. Whisk together until well combined. Reserve one-third in a bowl covered with plastic wrap for basting the next day. Pour the remaining marinade over the pork strips and gently rub with your hands to evenly coat them. Cover the pan with plastic wrap or zip up the bag. Transfer both the reserved marinade and the pork strips to the refrigerator overnight.

The next day, preheat the oven to 350°F. Fit a roasting pan with a rack that is at least 2 inches tall. Fill the pan with a ¼ inch of water. Lay the pork strips on the rack and roast for 20 minutes. Flip all of the strips over and baste with some of the reserved marinade. Roast for another 20 minutes. Flip all of the strips one more time and baste again before roasting for another 20 minutes. The pork should be just cooked through and still moist at the center. Transfer the strips to a wire rack set in a rimmed baking sheet to cool a bit. The pork can be served immediately or cooled completely before using for another recipe.

SPAM FRIED RICE

3 cups day-old cooked short-grain rice, at room temperature

1 tablespoon sesame oil

Neutral oil, for frying

Half 12-ounce can Spam Less Sodium, cut into ⅛ by 1-inch matchsticks

1 cup finely diced carrots (about 1½ carrots)

1 cup finely diced Maui or yellow onion (about ½ onion)

Kosher salt and freshly ground black pepper

1 cup chopped green onions, white and green parts (about 4 green onions)

1 teaspoon very finely grated garlic (about 2 cloves)

1 tablespoon soy sauce (shoyu)

1 tablespoon oyster sauce

1 teaspoon Worcestershire sauce

2 large eggs, lightly beaten

4 to 6 fried eggs, for serving (optional)

Serves 4 to 6

ON THE MENU:

Takuan, page 69

Side salad with Guava Dressing, page 219

Guava Cake, page 189

I'm not really a leftovers person. There, I said it—and to be clear, it's not that I don't eat them. I'd just rather eat something new every night. However, if fried rice is ever on the table, I am almost always the first one to dive into it. To me, it's one of the best ways to enjoy leftovers because it makes them new again. Forgotten veggies, day-old rice, and leftover meats are all fair game. And this version, the Spam version, is great if you haven't got any leftover meat on hand. Every culture—scratch that—every household has its own take on the ultimate fried rice, but this is the one I grew up with. If you're a fried rice purist and believe it should be just carrots, onions, and Spam, stick to this recipe. If you're more adventurous, add whatever you've got on hand, like frozen peas, chopped chicken or steak, or even the green beans you made the other night. I highly recommend serving this with a fried egg on top and maybe even a dollop of ketchup or sriracha sauce. People have been known to add mayo, which isn't anything I've tried, but to each their own.

In a bowl, combine the rice and sesame oil, toss to coat, and set aside.

Set a wide pan or wok over medium heat and coat the bottom with 1 to 2 teaspoons neutral oil. Fry the Spam for a minute on each side, or until all sides are lightly crisped and brown. Transfer the Spam to a small bowl and set aside.

Turn the heat to medium-low and coat the bottom of the pan with 1 to 2 tablespoons neutral oil. Once the oil is shimmering and hot, add the carrots and Maui onion and stir-fry with a wooden spoon or spatula until mostly translucent, 4 to 5 minutes. Season with salt and pepper before increasing the heat to medium. Add ½ cup of the green onions and cook for another minute to soften them. Add the rice, garlic, soy sauce, oyster sauce, Worcestershire sauce, and Spam, mixing and breaking up the rice with the spoon. Stir-fry until the rice is hot and has absorbed all of the liquids, 4 to 5 minutes. Taste and add more salt and pepper, if needed.

Create a well in the middle of the rice and pour in the eggs. Let sit for 30 seconds before scrambling the mixture, using the wooden spoon, for another 30 seconds. Let sit for 30 seconds more, then scramble again, this time bringing in the walls of rice and incorporating them into the eggs. Repeat this process until the eggs have been thoroughly scrambled and incorporated. Turn off the heat, leaving the pan to sit until you are ready to serve. Sprinkle with the remaining ½ cup green onions and serve, topping each serving wit a fried egg, if desired.

SOY-GLAZED SPAM MUSUBI

2 tablespoons soy sauce (shoyu)

2 tablespoons light brown sugar

½ teaspoon mirin (optional)

1 to 2 teaspoons neutral oil

One 12-ounce can Spam Less Sodium, cut horizontally into 8 slices

3 sheets roasted sushi nori, cut into thirds crosswise

2 teaspoons furikake (see page 31)

5 to 6 cups cooked short-grain rice

Makes 8 musubi

ON THE MENU:

Boiled Peanuts, page 205

Manapua, page 197

Pickled Mango, page 194

It's true: people from Hawai'i consume more Spam than the rest of the United States of America. Locals developed a taste for it during World War II and never lost it. It's endured for decades due to its salty flavor, versatility, and, partly, nostalgia and pride. If you've never had it, it's essentially a very salty, compressed ham that, yes, comes in a can. It's packaged similarly to gefilte fish, with that same clear, gelatinous fluid. And it's delicious.

We add it to our fried rice, saimin, and cold somen salads and serve it for breakfast with eggs and rice. But the most iconic way we dish it up is in this very portable musubi form. It's a play on the Japanese o-musubi and onigiri, which are both basically a ball of rice wrapped in nori. You can find it at the local 7-Eleven, mom-and-pop shops, and local diners, but it's best when it's freshly made. Whether you keep it simple and fry it without a glaze, sandwich it in between two mounds of rice instead of stacking it atop one mound, cover it with a wide or narrow strip of nori, or even add a strip of fried egg to it, the truth remains that this is a must-try. And if Spam is not your jam, you can always substitute a piece of Mochiko Chicken (page 100), a tonkatsu steak, or even some Teriyaki Beef Sticks (page 119). Spam musubi maker molds can be purchased from Amazon.

In a small bowl, whisk the soy sauce, brown sugar, and mirin (if using) together. Set aside.

Lightly coat the bottom of a large skillet with the oil and heat over medium heat. Fry the Spam slices until evenly browned and crispy, 2 to 3 minutes on each side. Turn the heat to low for the last minute of cooking, then turn off the heat. Pour in the soy mixture and quickly turn the Spam slices to evenly coat them. The mixture will cook down in less than a minute, so don't walk away for this part or your glaze may burn. Immediately transfer the Spam slices, with glaze, to a plate.

Place a strip of nori, rough side up, on a cutting board or clean work surface. Place the Spam musubi maker mold over it, in the middle, then place a slice of Spam in the mold. Alternatively, if you don't have a mold, you can line a cleaned Spam can with plastic wrap instead. Sprinkle ¼ teaspoon furikake over the Spam, then fill the mold with a generous mound of rice. Press the rice firmly with the musubi maker press until it is ¾ to 1 inch thick, adding more rice as necessary. Use the press to hold the rice down with one hand and pull the mold upward to unmold the musubi with your other hand. If you're using the Spam can, simply pull the plastic wrap from the can to unmold. Wrap the nori around the Spam-rice stack, bringing both ends of the strip to the middle, folding one over the other, and flipping it over so the seam is down and the Spam is facing up. Repeat with remaining ingredients. Serve immediately or wrap with plastic wrap to take with you on the go.

PORK VINHA D'ALHOS

2 teaspoons Hawaiian salt ('alaea)

5 garlic cloves, peeled and finely grated

2 pounds pork butt, with fat cap, cut into 2-inch cubes with fat on

1 cup apple cider vinegar

2 cups water

1 tablespoon whole black peppercorns

2 bay leaves

2 Hawaiian chili peppers (nīoi), thinly sliced

2 russet potatoes, peeled and cut into 2-inch cubes

Neutral oil, for frying

Flaky salt and freshly ground black pepper

Serves 4 to 6

ON THE MENU:

Pickled Onion, page 67

Side salad with Papaya Seed Dressing, page 218

Pie Crust Manju, page 179

Say "ving-a-dosh"! My boyfriend's mother makes this dish, Portuguese pickled pork, every Easter Sunday, Christmas, and New Year's Day for breakfast. Her recipe was passed down orally by her mother, and her mother's mother passed it down the same way. Up until recently, they had never written it out! While I've taken some liberties, the heart of the recipe is hers. Serve this with a fried egg, steamed white rice, and some Pickled Onion (page 67).

Massage the salt and grated garlic into the pork butt cubes. In a large bowl or a gallon-size freezer ziplock bag, combine the pork with the vinegar, water, peppercorns, bay leaves, and chili peppers. Cover the bowl with plastic wrap or seal the ziplock bag and transfer to the refrigerator to marinate overnight. In the morning, stir gently or flip the bag before stirring in the potatoes. Return to the refrigerator to marinate for at least 3 hours, or until you are ready to cook.

Line a rimmed baking sheet with paper towels and set aside. In a large pot, bring the pork and marinade to a boil over high heat, reserving the potatoes. When the liquid comes to a boil, skim off any scum that floats to the surface with a skimmer or slotted spoon, turn the heat to low, and cover the pot with a lid. Simmer for 30 minutes, skimming the scum off the top as needed. Add the potatoes and continue to simmer, with the lid on, for another 30 minutes. Remove the pork and potatoes from the liquid with a slotted spoon, placing them on the paper towel–lined rimmed baking sheet.

Line a large plate with paper towels and set aside. In a large skillet, heat enough oil to coat the bottom over medium-high heat. When the oil is shiny and shimmering, crisp the pork and potatoes, in batches, on all sides. This goes quickly, and you should need only a minute or two on each side. The pieces should be uniformly golden and crispy. Place the crisp, golden pieces on the prepared plate and immediately season with flaky salt and black pepper to taste. Repeat until everything has been panfried. Serve immediately.

PORK AND PEAS

1½ pounds pork butt, with fat cap

1 teaspoon neutral oil

1 small Maui onion, peeled and sliced into ½-inch wedges

2 garlic cloves, peeled and finely minced

½ red bell pepper, seeded and cut into ½-inch-wide strips

½ teaspoon Hawaiian salt ('alaea)

1 teaspoon freshly ground black pepper

1 tablespoon cane vinegar, coconut vinegar, or apple cider vinegar

1 tablespoon soy sauce (shoyu)

One 15-ounce can tomato sauce

2 vine-ripened tomatoes, seeded and diced into ½-inch cubes

2 bay leaves

1 cinnamon stick

1 cup frozen peas

3 cups steamed rice, for serving

Serves 4 to 6

ON THE MENU:

Side salad with Creamy Asian Dressing, page 217

Lumpia, page 48

Cascaron, page 180

Pork guisantes, or pork and peas, is a simple yet hearty dish that's usually made by stewing pork, peas, and bell peppers in tomato sauce. It comes together quickly and is well balanced with warm notes of cinnamon, bright and tangy flavors, and a touch of soy. This is a great weeknight meal and tastes even better when it's reheated the next day.

Trim the fat cap from the pork, cut the cap into a couple pieces, and set aside. Slice the lean pork meat into 1 by 1½ by ½-inch strips.

In a large skillet over medium heat, cook the trimmed pork fat until golden brown and the fat has rendered, 3 to 4 minutes on each side. Remove the fat cap pieces from the pan and discard. Add the oil to the pan and heat over medium heat until shiny, then add the onion and turn the heat to medium-low. Sauté until the onion has softened and is nearly translucent, 4 to 5 minutes. Add the lean pork strips, garlic, and bell pepper and cook until the pork is browned on both sides, another 5 to 6 minutes. Season with the salt and black pepper. Add the vinegar and soy sauce and cook for 2 minutes, stirring often, before adding the tomato sauce, tomatoes, bay leaves, and cinnamon stick. Simmer on low heat until the pork is tender, about 45 minutes. You can test this by sticking a fork in it; if the fork can be easily inserted, it's done.

Remove the cinnamon stick and bay leaves. Stir in the frozen peas and cook until they are heated through, another minute or two. Serve with steamed rice.

PORTUGUESE BEAN SOUP

1½ to 2 pounds smoked pork shanks

One 28-ounce can crushed tomatoes

One 8-ounce can tomato sauce

2 tablespoons ketchup, (preferably Heinz)

4 or 5 garlic cloves, peeled and finely grated

2 teaspoons portuguese spice blend (see page 73)

Kosher salt and freshly ground black pepper

3 or 4 carrots, peeled and sliced crosswise into ¼-inch-thick rounds

3 or 4 celery stalks, sliced thinly at an angle

1 Maui onion, diced

2 russet potatoes, peeled and cut into ¾-inch cubes

One 5-ounce Portuguese sausage, thinly sliced, or 5 ounces cooked Portuguese Sausage Patties (page 73), broken into bite-size pieces

Two 15-ounce cans red kidney beans, drained

1 cup coarsely chopped fresh cilantro

1 bunch dinosaur or lacinto kale, tough stems removed, cut into chiffonade (thin ribbons)

Serves 6 to 8

ON THE MENU:

Cornbread, page 74
Pohole Fern Salad, page 62
Haupia, page 168

My boyfriend, Moses, comes from a big Hawaiian family on both sides. His mom's side is Hawaiian Portuguese and they have carried on the family's culinary traditions. Growing up, his parents would make a huge pot of soup, and everyone would eat it over the course of the next few days for breakfast, lunch, or dinner, but always with lots of white rice.

On the surface, this soup may appear humble and unassuming, but it's meaty and hearty, loaded with spices, herbs, and, yes, a touch of ketchup, which Moses says is the secret ingredient. Most recipes call for cabbage, but I prefer the toothsome bite and brightness that kale adds to the soup. Cooked low and slow, this soup is made for cold days and family meals.

In a large pot, cover the smoked pork shanks with water by 1 inch. Bring the water to a boil over high heat. Cover with a lid, turn the heat to low, and simmer for 2 hours. Be sure to skim off the foam as needed. Add the tomatoes, tomato sauce, ketchup, garlic, spice blend, salt and pepper to taste, carrots, celery, onion, and potatoes and bring to a boil over medium-high heat. Turn the heat to low, cover, and simmer for another hour. Taste the soup and adjust the seasoning as desired.

In a skillet, over medium heat, fry the Portuguese sausage for 3 to 4 minutes, until browned. Add the fried sausage, kidney beans, cilantro, and kale to the soup and cook for 10 minutes more. Ladle the soup into bowls and serve. Store any leftovers covered in the pot, or in an airtight container, in the refrigerator for up to 3 days.

CUSTOMER
PARKING
ONLY

NO OVERNIGHT PARKING

VIOLATORS WILL BE TOWED
AT DRIVER/OWNERS EXPENSE

FOR TOWED VEHICLES CALL:

D & D TOWING
(808) 871-1185

HRS SEC. 290-11

CHICKEN

(Moa)

This chapter is a great place to trace your way through the multifaceted fabric of Hawai'i's local food culture. From braised Chicken Adobo (page 107) and Shoyu Chicken (page 103) to fried Chicken Katsu (page 111), it's easy to taste the many different cooking methods that came over to the islands so many years ago.

MOCHIKO CHICKEN

2 pounds boneless, skinless chicken thighs

¼ cup mochiko flour (see page 28)

¼ cup cornstarch

¼ cup sugar

¼ cup soy sauce (shoyu)

½ teaspoon kosher salt

2 large eggs, beaten

¼ cup chopped green onions, both white and green parts (about 4 green onions), plus more for garnish

Neutral oil, for frying

2 garlic cloves, peeled and extra finely grated

3 to 4 sheets nori, cut into 1-inch wide strips (optional)

3 cups steamed rice, for serving

Serves 6 to 8

ON THE MENU:

Namasu, page 68
Dynamite Sauce, page 217
Ice Cake, page 175

There's nothing quite like fried chicken. It's crispy on the outside, juicy on the inside, and, when done right, packed with flavor. I think it's safe to say that most places have their own version, and Hawai'i is no exception. This sweet rice flour–battered chicken is perfectly crunchy, salty-sweet, and highly addictive. It's one of my all-time favorite dishes, and I'm taken back to my childhood every single time I have it. While I believe it's best served warm with onigiri (aka triangle-shaped musubi), Namasu (page 68), and Takuan (page 69), the way my mom serves it, it's equally great cold, chopped up, and tossed into a green salad with Creamy Asian Dressing (page 217) or atop a bed of cold somen noodles.

Cut the chicken thighs into 2-inch-long strips and place them in a bowl. In a small bowl, combine the mochiko, cornstarch, sugar, soy sauce, salt, eggs, green onions, and garlic, and whisk until fully combined. Pour the batter mixture over the chicken and mix to coat evenly. Marinate in the refrigerator for at least 5 hours, preferably overnight.

Line a baking sheet with paper towels or newspaper and place a wire rack on top. Fill a Dutch oven or high-sided pot with oil to a depth of 2 inches and heat over medium-low heat to 330° to 340°F. Remove the chicken from the bowl and wrap each piece with a strip of nori (if using).

Without crowding the pot, add as many pieces of chicken as you can to the hot oil; the temperature will drop to between 315° and 325°F when you add the chicken. Fry the chicken for 6 to 7 minutes, turning with a skimmer or long chopsticks to brown evenly. The chicken will be golden brown when it's done and the internal temperature should be 165°F. Remove with a skimmer or long chopsticks and let cool on the wire rack for 8 to 10 minutes. Continue this process until all the chicken has been cooked. When ready to serve, garnish with freshly chopped green onions and serve with rice.

SHOYU CHICKEN

¾ cup soy sauce (shoyu)

1½ cups water

2 tablespoons honey

½ cup packed dark brown sugar

One 2-inch piece fresh ginger, peeled and thinly sliced

2 or 3 garlic cloves, peeled and crushed

2 pounds bone-in, skin-on chicken thighs

½ Maui onion, peeled and cut into ¾-inch wedges

2 or 3 green onions, white and green parts, cut into 2-inch pieces

1½ tablespoons cornstarch

3 cups steamed rice, for serving

Serves 4 to 6

ON THE MENU:

Takuan, page 69

Side salad with Creamy Asian Dressing, page 217

Macadamia Nut Cream Pie, page 164

One of my favorite plate lunch options, shoyu chicken will forever hold a special place in my heart because it reminds me of my uncle Johnson and aunty Vicki, owners of Surfside Deli in Kīhei, Maui. (It is a common sign of respect in Hawai'i to call elders "aunty" or "uncle"; we're not actually related.) Surfside is a local-style deli, meaning they do not serve lox and bagels and are not known for their sandwiches, instead serving up plate lunches to surfers, construction workers, and anyone who happens to be nearby and hungry! Shoyu chicken is their number-one seller, and for that reason, I cannot think about this perfectly balanced sweet, salty, umami-packed chicken without thinking of Uncle Johnson and Aunty Vicki.

In addition to rice, serve this with Mac Salad (page 55) and some pickles, like Takuan (page 69), if desired.

In a heavy Dutch oven or pot, mix the soy sauce, water, honey, brown sugar, ginger, and garlic together. Nestle the chicken thighs in the sauce, skin side up, submerging the meat as much as possible. Bring the mixture to a boil over medium-high heat. When the sauce comes to a boil, add the Maui onion wedges and green onion pieces and turn the heat to medium-low. Cover the pot with a lid and let simmer for 30 minutes. Using a pair of kitchen tongs, gently turn all the chicken pieces over. Cover the pot again and simmer for another 30 minutes. Check the tenderness of the meat with a fork; if you can easily insert the fork into the meat, the chicken is done. Remove the cooked thighs from the sauce, reserving it, and place them on a rimmed baking sheet.

Preheat the broiler.

In a small bowl, whisk the cornstarch with ¼ cup of the sauce until smooth, then add the cornstarch mixture back to the pot with the remaining sauce and cook over medium-low for 4 to 5 minutes, until the sauce has thickened. Broil the chicken thighs for a minute or two, watching carefully to make sure you do not burn the skin. The goal is to just quickly brown the skin.

Serve the chicken with the thickened sauce and rice.

CHICKEN JOOK

1 small rotisserie chicken carcass and any leftover meat

One 2-inch piece fresh ginger, thinly sliced

4 garlic cloves, peeled and smashed

½ Maui onion, unpeeled

4½ quarts water

2 cups uncooked short-grain rice

Hawaiian salt ('alaea)

Fried garlic, for serving

Crispy fried onions, for serving

Coarsely chopped fresh cilantro, for serving

Thinly sliced green onions, white and green parts, for serving

Soy sauce (shoyu), for serving

Sriracha, for serving

Serves 4 to 6

ON THE MENU:

Takuan, page 69

Pickled Onion, page 67

Ice Cake, page 175

Sometimes called congee or rice porridge, jook is a soup that Chinese plantation workers introduced to the islands. Often made these days with turkey following Thanksgiving, jook is a comforting dish that's great for cold winter nights, rainy days, or when you're feeling under the weather. I make it whenever I have roasted a chicken or pick up a rotisserie chicken from the store.

In a large stockpot, cover the chicken carcass, ginger, garlic, and onion with the water and bring to a boil over high heat. Turn the heat to low and simmer for 2 hours, covering with the lid after 1 hour. Remove and discard the carcass, reserving any pieces of meat, and strain the stock through a fine-mesh sieve into another large stockpot.

Set the stock over high heat and add the rice and reserved meat. Bring it to a boil, then turn the heat to medium-low and simmer for 15 minutes, stirring often. Turn the heat to low and simmer for 1½ hours, stirring every 10 to 15 minutes to prevent the rice from sticking to the bottom. Taste the jook and season with Hawaiian salt. The jook is ready when the rice is broken down and the soup is thickened. It should resemble porridge or oatmeal.

Ladle the jook into bowls and top with fried garlic, crispy fried onions, cilantro, green onions, soy sauce, and sriracha, all to taste, before serving.

CHICKEN ADOBO

3 bay leaves

4 teaspoons whole black peppercorns

1 tablespoon neutral oil

1½ pounds bone-in, skin-on chicken thighs

1½ pounds skin-on chicken wings or drumettes

½ cup cane vinegar, coconut vinegar, or apple cider vinegar

½ cup soy sauce (shoyu)

½ cup lager beer

1 tablespoon brown sugar

5 garlic cloves, peeled and smashed

3 cups steamed rice, for serving (optional)

Serves 6 to 8

ON THE MENU:

Namasu, page 68

Side salad with Guava Dressing, page 219

Double-Chocolate Haupia Pie, page 163

I like to think of chicken adobo, one of the best-known Filipino dishes, as the Filipino cousin of Shoyu Chicken (page 103). Both are braised, well balanced, and packed with flavor; however, chicken adobo is marked by its tanginess, while shoyu chicken's flavor is decidedly sweeter. Whether or not you agree with me, I think we can all acknowledge chicken adobo is delicious. While not exactly traditional, thanks to the added beer, this is my take on the unofficial national dish of the Philippines. You can substitute pork butt for the chicken; simply cut the pork into 2-inch cubes.

In a medium Dutch oven or pot set over medium heat, toast the bay leaves and the black peppercorns until everything is very fragrant and the bay leaves have a sheen (they start out dull), 3 to 4 minutes. Remove the spices from the heat. Crush three-quarters of the black peppercorns with a mortar and pestle or a grinder before setting them aside with the remaining peppercorns and bay leaves to use later. Return the Dutch oven to the stove top and add the oil. Heat over medium heat until shiny and shimmering, add as much chicken as will fit, and brown it in batches, skin side down, until the fat has rendered and the skin is golden brown, 6 to 8 minutes. Wiggle the pieces around from time to time to prevent their skin from sticking. There's no need to flip them midway as you are only browning the skin side of the thighs and one side of the wings. Transfer the browned chicken to a plate and repeat the process until all the chicken has been browned. After you've browned it all, remove the pot from the heat and pour out the excess oil and rendered fat, reserving 1 tablespoon for the sauce.

Return the pot to the stove top with the reserved tablespoon of rendered fat and add the vinegar, soy sauce, beer, brown sugar, garlic, and the toasted bay leaves and black peppercorns. Cook over low heat for 2 minutes, stirring with a wooden spoon to combine. Add the chicken and any juices back to the pot and increase the heat to medium-high to bring the sauce to a low boil. Then turn the heat to medium-low, cover the pot with a lid, and simmer for 45 minutes, flipping the chicken once halfway through. Remove the lid and continue simmering for another 15 minutes. Remove the chicken from the sauce and place it, skin side up, on a rimmed baking sheet.

Turn the heat up to high and let the sauce cook at a rapid boil until it has been reduced by more than half, 5 to 6 minutes.

Meanwhile, preheat the broiler. Broil the chicken pieces for 5 minutes. Remove the chicken from the oven and return the chicken pieces back to the pot, flipping them once to coat both sides with sauce. Serve with the hot rice, if desired, spooning on some of the sauce.

LOCAL-STYLE BBQ CHICKEN

½ cup ketchup

½ cup soy sauce (shoyu)

½ cup packed brown sugar

¼ cup rice vinegar

One 1-inch piece fresh ginger, peeled and finely grated

2 garlic cloves, peeled and finely grated

3 pounds boneless, skinless chicken thighs

Serves 6 to 8

ON THE MENU:

Namasu, page 68

Mac Salad, page 55

Butter Mochi, page 167

Come fund-raising season, you'll start to see a lot of people selling tickets for huli huli chicken. Huli huli, which translates to "turn turn," is a local-style barbecue chicken that is grilled and basted on a spit. The sweet marinade burns a bit, so I recommend you grill outside to avoid smoking up your house and setting off the fire alarms!

In a large bowl, whisk together the ketchup, soy sauce, brown sugar, rice vinegar, ginger, and garlic until well combined. Reserve ⅓ cup of the mixture for later. To the remaining mixture, add the chicken and stir to evenly coat it. You can transfer this mixture with the chicken to a gallon-size ziplock bag or simply cover the bowl with plastic wrap. Refrigerate for at least 8 hours or overnight, turning the chicken at least once.

After marinating the chicken, oil your grill grates well. Heat the grill to medium and grill the chicken for 5 to 7 minutes on each side, until cooked through, basting it with the reserved marinade after you turn it. Serve immediately.

CHICKEN KATSU

Katsu Sauce

½ cup ketchup

3 tablespoons Worcestershire sauce

1 tablespoon soy sauce (shoyu)

1 tablespoon mirin

2 teaspoons sugar

Pinch of garlic powder

¾ pound boneless, skinless chicken breasts, halved and pounded to ¼-inch thickness

¾ teaspoon kosher salt

½ teaspoon freshly ground black pepper

⅛ teaspoon granulated garlic

¼ cup all-purpose flour

2 large eggs, beaten

1½ to 2 cups panko bread crumbs

Neutral oil, for frying

Serves 4 to 6

ON THE MENU:

Takuan, page 69

Namasu, page 68

Guava Cake, page 189

When I was in elementary school, one of my best friends was Kira, my next-door neighbor. Her dad, Uncle Milton, made the best chicken katsu, and I remember crossing my fingers that he'd make us lunch when we played at her house on the weekends or during the summer. What I loved about it was that garlicky flavor, which I now know was from garlic salt. I made my own using a combination of kosher salt and granulated garlic. This panko-crusted chicken is a popular plate-lunch item and is found at most restaurants, but I'm telling you, they're missing the secret ingredient!

To make the katsu sauce, whisk together the ketchup, Worcestershire sauce, soy sauce, mirin, sugar, and garlic powder in a small bowl until the sugar has dissolved. Cover the bowl with plastic wrap and store in the refrigerator until ready to use.

Evenly season the chicken breasts on both sides with the salt, pepper, and garlic. Place the flour, eggs, and panko into three separate shallow dishes. Coat the chicken breasts in the flour, shaking off any excess flour. Next, dip them into the eggs, allowing any excess to drip off before pressing them into the panko, coating both sides well. Place the pieces on a plate.

Line a plate with paper towels and set aside. In a large skillet, heat ¼ inch of oil over medium heat until it's shiny. Working in batches, cook the chicken in the hot oil until golden, 3 to 4 minutes on each side. Set on the paper towel-lined plate to drain. Repeat until all the chicken has been fried. Serve immediately with the katsu sauce.

BEEF

(Pipi)

From soups to stews to patties smothered in gravy, local Hawaiians have found many ways to cook with beef. If you've walked through any Hawai'i beach park, you'll be familiar with the sweet smell of Maui-Style Kalbi Short Ribs (page 120) charring on the grill. And if you've been to a local potluck, you know why Beef Chili (page 128) is a must.

LOCO MOCO

1 pound 80/20 or 85/15 ground beef

1 teaspoon kosher salt, plus more as needed

½ teaspoon freshly ground black pepper, plus more as needed

3 teaspoons Worcestershire sauce

1 medium Maui or yellow onion; ¼ chopped, and ¾ sliced into ½-inch wedges

2 garlic cloves, peeled and finely grated

2½ tablespoons neutral oil

8 ounces cremini mushrooms, cleaned and sliced

Salt and freshly ground black pepper

2 cups beef broth

2 teaspoons soy sauce (shoyu)

1 tablespoon cornstarch

4 cups steamed white rice

4 large eggs, fried sunny-side up or over easy

2 chopped green onions, green parts only, for garnish

Serves 4

ON THE MENU:

Mac Salad, page 55

Side salad with Papaya Seed Dressing, page 218

Butter Mochi, page 167

The great debate on the Big Island of Hawai'i is who invented the loco moco. Some will tell you that Lincoln Grill was the first to make it; others will swear it was Café 100. Legend has it that a bunch of teenagers nicknamed it "loco moco" after a guy they called "Crazy George." So what is it? Loco moco is similar to a Japanese dish called hambāgu, or hamburger steak, which consists of a panfried ground-meat patty served with a tangy-sweet sauce and white rice. The loco moco takes this one step further, throwing the patty over rice, then smothering it in a brown gravy and topping it with a sunny-side up egg.

This is a breakfast, lunch, or dinner kind of dish. In Hawai'i, you can order it at any time of day, and it's an epic hangover or late-night meal (not that I'd know). So if you've got the midnight munchies, or simply want a hearty breakfast, lunch, or dinner, get to work! George's loco moco awaits you.

In a bowl combine the ground beef, salt, pepper, 1½ teaspoons of the Worcestershire sauce, chopped onion, and garlic. Gently mix with your hands or a wooden spoon until just combined, being careful not to overmix. Form into four equal-size patties about ½ inch thick. Place the patties on a plate, cover with plastic wrap, and transfer to the refrigerator to rest for 20 minutes.

While the patties are resting, add 1 tablespoon of the oil to a large skillet set over medium heat. When the oil is hot (shiny and shimmering), add the onion wedges and sauté until almost translucent, 5 to 7 minutes. Turn the heat to low and continue cooking for 10 minutes, stirring often. Cook until they are soft and caramelized; you should be able to smell the sugar. Transfer to a bowl and set aside.

Add another 1 tablespoon of the oil to the skillet and set it over medium heat. When the oil is hot, swirl the pan around to evenly coat it, then gently place the patties in the pan, leaving room around each one. Cook until browned, about 4 minutes on each side. Using a spatula, remove the patties and transfer to a clean plate to rest.

Add the remaining ½ tablespoon oil to the pan and heat over medium heat until hot. Add the mushrooms and sauté until tender, about 10 minutes. Season the mushrooms with salt and pepper, then add the reserved caramelized onions. Add the beef broth, soy sauce, and the remaining 1½ teaspoons Worcestershire sauce and bring to a simmer. Turn the heat to medium-low, scoop out a tablespoon of the broth from the skillet, and whisk it with the cornstarch in a small bowl until smooth. Whisk the cornstarch slurry into the skillet and simmer until the sauce has thickened, 5 to 7 minutes.

Place 1 cup steamed rice on each plate and top (in this order) with 1 patty, some gravy, 1 fried egg, and chopped green onions before serving.

OXTAIL
SOUP

You probably wouldn't guess it, but Hawai'i is one of the nation's top consumers of oxtails. You can get oxtail soup in restaurants all over the islands, but the dipping sauce from the Alley Restaurant in Aiea Bowl on the island of O'ahu is the one I dream about—and it was featured on Guy Fieri's *Diners, Drive-Ins and Dives*. Plan ahead when making this soup, as it requires 2 days' time.

4 to 5 pounds oxtail

4 cups beef broth

2 cups chicken broth

3 whole star anise

One 2-inch piece fresh ginger, peeled and thinly sliced

6 dried shiitake mushrooms

4 pieces dried mandarin peel (from 1 orange; see Note)

1 tablespoon Hawaiian salt ('alaea)

1 cup raw peanuts, skinned

Sauce

¼ cup peeled and grated fresh ginger, drained

½ cup peeled and finely grated daikon radish (solids and juice)

⅓ cup light soy sauce (shoyu)

¼ cup fresh lemon juice

½ teaspoon sesame oil

1½ teaspoons sambal oelek

To Serve

1 bunch fresh cilantro, leaves and stems, coarsely chopped

1 bunch green onions, white and green parts, chopped

8 to 10 baby bok choy, blanched and flashed in cold water

½ head napa cabbage (won bok), shredded

3 cups steamed rice

Serves 4 to 6

ON THE MENU:

Fried Wontons, page 41

Pickled Onion, page 67

Liliko'i Chiffon Pie, page 159

Fill a large pot halfway with water and bring to a boil. Cut the oxtails into segments and parboil for 30 minutes. Drain the oxtails and rinse in water to remove any scum. Let cool slightly before using a sharp knife to trim away all excess fat.

Return the cleaned and trimmed oxtails to the pot and add the beef and chicken broths. Add water to cover the oxtails by 2 inches. Add the star anise, ginger, mushrooms, mandarin peel, and salt and bring to a boil over high heat. Turn the heat to medium, cover, and simmer for 2 hours.

Skim any scum off the top, add the peanuts, cover, and continue to simmer for another 2 hours. The oxtail meat should be tender and falling off the bone after 4 hours total. If it isn't, continue boiling, with the lid on, until it is. At this point, remove the pot from the heat and let the soup cool to room temperature. Transfer to the refrigerator to chill overnight. This does two things: it allows the fat to float to the top and solidify, and it gives the aromatics a chance to infuse the broth and oxtails.

In the morning, or an hour before you're ready to serve, remove the pot from the refrigerator and skim off the solidified fat. Heat the pot of soup, with the lid on, over medium heat until it comes to a moderate boil. If desired, remove the shiitake mushrooms from the soup and remove the stems with a sharp knife. Slice the mushrooms thinly and return to the soup.

To make the sauce, meanwhile combine the ginger, daikon, soy sauce, lemon juice, sesame oil, and sambal oelek in a small bowl. Be sure to taste it and adjust the flavors to your liking.

To serve, ladle the oxtails and broth into large bowls. Garnish the bowls with cilantro, green onions, baby bok choy, and napa cabbage (or any other toppings you'd prefer). Serve with individual bowls of hot white rice and individual bowls of the sauce, which can be used to dip the meat into or poured right into the broth!

Note: To make dried mandarin peel, score an organic mandarin orange into quarters, remove the peel, and use a sharp paring knife to separate the peel from the white pith. Set out the peel to dry in a sunny spot for 1 week before using. Alternatively, peels can be placed on a rimmed baking sheet and dried in an oven set to the lowest temperature for 3 hours, until curled and dried. Any type of mandarin, including tangerines, satsumas, and the like, can be used.

TERIYAKI BEEF STICKS

1 cup soy sauce (shoyu)

1 cup sugar

3 tablespoons mirin

4 garlic cloves, peeled and finely minced or grated

One 1½-inch piece fresh ginger, peeled and finely grated

1½ pounds flank steak, thinly sliced across the grain into long strips

3 cups steamed rice, for serving

Serves 4 to 6

ON THE MENU:

Pickled Onion, page 67
Saimin, page 143
Pie Crust Manju, page 179

My childhood field trips usually included these sticks. Tucked away in layers of foil, cuddled up next to salty triangle musubi, and packed with a pouch of Capri Sun, my lunches were always the envy of my class. Beef teriyaki is a staple of the plate-lunch menu in Hawai'i, as it is very versatile (you can broil, panfry, or grill it) and takes almost no time to prepare. You simply whisk together a quick five-ingredient marinade of soy sauce, sugar, mirin, garlic, and ginger. On any given Sunday, you'll smell it before you see it on the grill at every beach park in the state and most certainly on every family potluck table.

While each family has its own tip or trick or perfect ratio, this one is a good starting point for your own recipe. Depending on the brand of soy sauce you use, there may be some trial and error to find your preferred marinating time. Start with 4 to 5 hours and fry up a little test batch. This is an especially good weeknight dish, as you can prepare it the night before and quickly panfry it the next day. Whatever you do, don't forget the rice (possibly formed into a triangle musubi) and pickled veggies, like Namasu (page 68) or Takuan (page 69)!

In a bowl, whisk the soy sauce, sugar, mirin, garlic, and ginger until combined. Add the meat and evenly coat with the marinade. Cover the bowl with plastic wrap and marinate the meat in the refrigerator for 2 to 3 hours. Meanwhile, soak 8 bamboo skewers in water for at least 1 hour before using, weighing them down with a heavy bowl.

Preheat the broiler.

Line a rimmed baking sheet with foil, dull side up, and spray lightly with oil. Thread the meat onto the skewers and set them on the baking sheet. Broil until the meat is browned and cooked through, 1 to 2 minutes on each side.

Serve with steamed rice.

MAUI-STYLE KALBI SHORT RIBS

2 cups soy sauce (shoyu)

1¼ cups water

¾ cup rice vinegar

1 tablespoon sesame oil

1½ tablespoons fish sauce

3½ cups packed dark brown sugar

One 4-inch piece fresh ginger, peeled and finely grated

5 garlic cloves, peeled and finely grated

6 pounds bone-in beef short ribs, ½-inch-thick flanken style (Korean or cross-cut), or 4 pounds boneless beef short ribs, ½-inch thick flanken style (Korean or cross-cut)

Toasted white sesame seeds, for garnish

A few green onions, white and green parts, chopped, for garnish

Serves 6 to 8; recipe can be halved

ON THE MENU:

Kim Chee, page 70

Side salad with Liliko'i Vinaigrette, page 218

Ice Cake, page 175

When I was a keiki (child), there was a place on Maui called Azeka's Ribs and Snack Shop, right down the street from my go-to boogie-boarding spot. I was never really that into boogie-boarding (though it was the cool thing at the time), but I did have a boogie board and we did go to this beach and pick up Azeka's famous marinated kalbi ribs afterward. Come to think of it, that's probably the only real reason I pretended to like boogie-boarding. For the ribs.

Sweet and tangy, these short ribs are my rendition of the famous "sweet meat" from Azeka's. While they can be broiled in the oven, they are best cooked on the grill. Just be sure to keep your eye on the grill, as this sweet meat can and will burn quickly if you're not watching it!

Serve with rice, sweet potatoes, and/or Potato Mac Salad (page 55).

In a bowl, whisk together the soy sauce, water, rice vinegar, sesame oil, fish sauce, brown sugar, ginger, and garlic until well combined. Divide the short ribs into two or three gallon-size ziplock bags and pour equal parts of the marinade into each bag. Refrigerate for at least 8 hours, though 24 hours is recommended for optimal flavor. Turn the bags at least three times during the marinating period.

Heat your grill to medium. Remove the ribs from the marinade and cook them to your desired doneness, 4 to 5 minutes on each side for medium-rare. If the ribs seem to be burning, adjust the heat to medium-low and cook for a minute or two longer on each side. Alternatively, you can broil them in the oven for 5 minutes on each side. Garnish the ribs with the toasted white sesame seeds and chopped green onions before serving.

Note: You can freeze half of the marinated ribs and grill them later; simply drain the marinade from the bag before freezing them.

MEAT JUN

2 pounds round steak, chuck steak, tri-tip steak, or flank steak

⅔ cup packed brown sugar

One 2-inch piece fresh ginger, peeled and grated

2 garlic cloves, peeled and finely grated

3 green onions, white and green parts, chopped

1 cup soy sauce (shoyu)

1 tablespoon toasted sesame seeds, ground

¼ cup sesame oil

1 teaspoon freshly ground black pepper

Dipping Sauce

¼ cup soy sauce (shoyu)

1 tablespoon gochujang

1 tablespoon rice vinegar

1½ tablespoons honey

1 teaspoon ground toasted sesame seeds

1 teaspoon sesame oil

½ teaspoon freshly ground black pepper

1 garlic clove, peeled and finely grated

One ½-inch piece fresh ginger, peeled and finely grated

2 green onions, thinly sliced

1 cup all-purpose flour

5 large eggs

Neutral oil, for frying

3 cups steamed rice, for serving

Serves 4 to 6

ON THE MENU:

Mandoo, page 47

Kim Chee, page 70

Shave Ice, page 172

There's a spot in Honolulu, O'ahu, called Gina's B-B-Q that I used to frequent in my early twenties more often than I'd like to admit. It's famous for Gina's Special mixed plate, which comes with kalbi short ribs, barbecue chicken, meat jun, three scoops of rice, and four sides. It was under $15 and fed me for days. Back then, the thought did not cross my mind to make my own meat jun; up until I met my boyfriend, I hadn't even tried. This recipe was adapted from his dad's secret family recipe.

Thinly cut the meat into ⅛-inch-thick slices and pound or tenderize them with a meat mallet in all directions.

In a bowl, combine the brown sugar, ginger, garlic, green onions, soy sauce, sesame seeds, sesame oil, and pepper and whisk together until well combined. Transfer this marinade to a gallon-size ziplock bag and add the meat. Transfer to the refrigerator and marinate the meat for 1 to 2 hours.

To make the dipping sauce, meanwhile, whisk together the soy sauce, gochujang, rice vinegar, honey, sesame seeds, sesame oil, pepper, garlic, ginger, and green onions in a small bowl.

Line a plate with paper towels and set aside. Place the flour in a shallow dish or bowl and beat the eggs in a second shallow dish or bowl. Add about ⅓ cup (or ¼ inch) of neutral oil to a large skillet and heat over medium-low heat until the oil is shiny and shimmering. Drain the meat, discarding the marinade, and set the meat in a dish. Working in batches, dredge the meat, one piece at a time, in the flour, shaking off the excess, then dip it into the egg, letting the excess drip off before placing each piece in the skillet. Fry until golden, 1 to 2 minutes on each side. Set on the paper towel-lined plate to drain. Repeat until all the meat has been fried.

Serve warm with the dipping sauce and steamed rice.

BEEF CURRY

1½ pounds beef chuck or other stew meat, cut into 1½-inch cubes

Kosher salt and freshly ground black pepper

6 tablespoons all-purpose flour

6 tablespoons unsalted butter

1 large or 2 small Maui or yellow onions, sliced into ½-inch wedges

3 garlic cloves, peeled and finely grated

2 teaspoons peeled and finely grated fresh ginger

⅔ cup red wine

1 cup 100 percent apple juice

3 tablespoons ketchup

1 tablespoon honey

2 tablespoons soy sauce (shoyu)

4 cups beef broth

3 carrots, peeled and sliced on the bias

2 russet potatoes, peeled and cut into 1½-inch cubes

4 celery stalks, sliced on the bias

2 teaspoons garam masala

1½ tablespoons curry powder

½ teaspoon instant espresso powder

¼ cup shredded Gouda

3 cups steamed rice, for serving

Serves 6 to 8

ON THE MENU:

Takuan, page 69

Side salad with Guava Dressing, page 219

Guava Cake, page 189

There's a saying in Hawai'i: "No worry, beef curry." It means "good to go, it's in the bag, it's all good, garanz ball baranz," or "garanz" for short. Basically, it means "guaranteed." And I can't tell you why or how beef curry and no worry came together—other than the fact that they rhyme—but I think it's safe to say that it's important enough to merit mention. The curry in Hawai'i is essentially Japanese. It's thick and stew-like and a little sweet like Japanese curry, but unlike traditional Japanese curry, it's loaded with meat, carrots, potatoes, onions, and sometimes celery. While most families pick up bricks of curry roux in the store, it doesn't take much more time to make this curry from scratch. Be sure to season with salt and pepper throughout the cooking process.

Season the stew meat with salt and pepper. Toss the meat with 2 tablespoons of the all-purpose flour, coating all sides evenly.

In a large Dutch oven or pot, heat 2 tablespoons of the unsalted butter over medium-high heat until it melts and just starts to sizzle. Add half the stew meat to the pan and cook until browned on all sides, about 5 minutes total. Remove the meat and set aside on a plate to rest. Add another 2 tablespoons of the butter to the pan and brown the second half of the meat for about 5 minutes more. Transfer to the plate and set aside.

Turn the heat to medium-low and, in the same pot, add the remaining 2 tablespoons butter and the onions and cook until the onions are translucent and slightly caramelized, about 10 minutes. Add the garlic and ginger and cook for 2 minutes. Add the red wine, apple juice, ketchup, honey, soy sauce, and beef broth and bring to a simmer. Add the browned beef and simmer for 30 minutes. Add the carrots, potatoes, and celery and simmer until the beef and vegetables are tender, about 30 minutes more. Add the garam masala, curry powder, and instant espresso powder and stir well.

Remove ¼ cup of the sauce from the pan and whisk it with the remaining 4 tablespoons flour before stirring it back into the pot. Cook for a few minutes to thicken the sauce, then stir in the Gouda. Serve with rice.

BEEF STEW

2½ pounds beef chuck or other stew meat, cut into 2-inch cubes

1 teaspoon Hawaiian salt ('alaea)

Freshly ground black pepper

4 to 5 tablespoons all-purpose flour

2 tablespoons neutral oil

1 cup finely diced Maui or yellow onion (½ onion), plus 1 Maui or yellow onion, sliced into ½-inch wedges

½ cup finely chopped celery leaves (from about 1 head of celery)

4 cups beef broth

One 8-ounce can tomato sauce

One 6-ounce can tomato paste

1 teaspoon Worcestershire sauce

2 teaspoons apple cider vinegar

2 bay leaves (optional)

2 garlic cloves, peeled and finely grated

Kosher salt

4 carrots, peeled and sliced on the bias into 1-inch-wide pieces

3 russet potatoes, peeled and cut into 1½-inch cubes

4 celery stalks, sliced on the bias into 1-inch-wide pieces

2 tablespoons mochiko flour (see page 28)

3 cups steamed rice or 1 recipe Cornbread (page 74), for serving

Serves 8

ON THE MENU:

Pickled Onion, page 67

Gau, page 186

Butter Mochi, page 167

This is a meal that was made for Sundays. It cooks low and slow, and it yields a large amount. While it's absolutely acceptable to halve the recipe, I think you'll find that you won't want to. Beef stew is almost always better the next day, especially when served over steamed white rice or with cornbread.

In a shallow bowl or dish, season the meat with the Hawaiian salt and 1 teaspoon pepper, then toss with 4 tablespoons of the all-purpose flour, adding another tablespoon if necessary, to evenly coat the meat.

Coat the bottom of a large, wide Dutch oven with the oil and heat over medium heat until shimmering. Brown the meat in batches, turning the meat to brown on all sides, and transfer to a plate when done. This should take 8 to 10 minutes per batch. Once all the meat has been browned, add it all to the Dutch oven along with the diced onion and celery leaves and cook for 5 minutes, stirring often. Stir in the beef broth, tomato sauce, tomato paste, Worcestershire sauce, vinegar, bay leaves (if using), and garlic and bring to a boil.

Cover and turn the heat to low; simmer until the meat is very tender, 1½ to 2 hours. Taste and adjust the seasoning with kosher salt and pepper as needed, add the carrots, and cook, with the lid on, for another hour. Next, add the onion wedges, potatoes, and celery and cook, with the lid on, until all the vegetables are tender, another 1 to 1½ hours. Taste the stew and adjust the seasoning.

In a small bowl, whisk the mochiko with ½ cup of the stew broth to make a slurry. Stir the slurry into the stew and cook, uncovered, for 10 minutes to cook the flour and thicken the stew. Serve with rice or cornbread.

BEEF CHILI

6 ounces bacon, chopped

2½ ounces Portuguese sausage, chopped, or cooked Portuguese Sausage Patties (page 73), broken into pieces

1 pound 93/7 ground beef

1 Maui onion, chopped

4 celery stalks, chopped

½ green bell pepper, seeded and chopped

3 garlic cloves, peeled and finely grated

½ teaspoon peeled and grated fresh ginger

¼ cup red wine

1 cup chicken broth

Two 8-ounce cans tomato sauce

2 bay leaves

1 teaspoon kosher salt

Freshly ground black pepper

2 teaspoons sugar

2 teaspoons chili powder

½ teaspoon dried oregano

Pinch of smoked paprika

¼ teaspoon ground cumin

1 teaspoon Worcestershire sauce

2 tablespoons ketchup

Two 15¼-oz cans kidney beans, rinsed and drained

1 to 2 tablespoons Best Foods (or Hellmann's) mayonnaise

3 cups steamed rice or 1 recipe Cornbread (page 74), for serving

Serves 6

ON THE MENU:

Fried Wontons, page 41

Side salad with Dynamite Sauce, page 217

Malasadas, page 183

Zippy's chili is renowned in the islands. It's sold in the freezer section of most grocery stores, and people buy buckets of it to take to potlucks. It's basically legendary. While the ingredient list for this recipe is lengthy, trust me when I say it's worth it. Both my boyfriend and my mother swear this is their new favorite chili. Serve it with steamed white rice or cornbread, and don't blame me if people start asking you to bring it to potlucks.

Line a plate with paper towels and set aside. In a large Dutch oven set over medium heat, fry the bacon and Portuguese sausage until crispy and browned, 5 to 6 minutes, stirring often with a wooden spoon. Remove with a slotted spoon and place on the paper towel–lined plate.

Add the ground beef to the pot and cook, stirring often and breaking up the meat into small pieces, until browned, 7 to 10 minutes. Remove the meat with a slotted spoon and place in a bowl. Drain all but 1 to 2 tablespoons fat from the pan.

Set the pot back over medium heat and add the onion, celery, bell pepper, garlic, and ginger. Cook until the onion is translucent and the celery is soft, 5 to 6 minutes, stirring frequently to prevent burning. Meanwhile, finely mince the fried bacon and Portuguese sausage. Once the onion is translucent, add the beef, bacon, and Portuguese sausage back into the pot. Add the red wine, chicken broth, tomato sauce, bay leaves, salt, black pepper to taste, sugar, chili powder, oregano, paprika, cumin, Worcestershire sauce, ketchup, and kidney beans. Stir with the wooden spoon to combine and bring to a low boil.

Turn the heat to low and simmer for 30 minutes; taste halfway through and adjust the seasoning. The liquid should reduce by at least half. If you like your chili thicker, continue simmering to the desired thickness. When you are ready to serve, remove the pot from the heat and mix in the mayonnaise to taste. Serve with rice or cornbread.

FROM THE SEA

(Mea'ai Kai)

When you're surrounded by water, you know a thing or two about preparing seafood. And oftentimes you know your fisherman and almost always where your seafood is coming from. While not everyone lives in Hawai'i, so close to fresh seafood, you can check with the Monterey Bay Aquarium Seafood Watch and search for sustainably sourced seafood to prepare the dishes in this chapter!

CHINESE-STYLE STEAMED FISH

1 tablespoon sesame oil

¼ cup soy sauce (shoyu)

2 teaspoons sugar

1 Hawaiian chili pepper (nīoi), thinly sliced (optional)

One 2-pound whole moi or other mild, white-fleshed fish, cleaned

Kosher salt and freshly ground black pepper

6 green onions, green parts only, cut into 2-inch lengths

One 3-inch piece fresh ginger, peeled and sliced crosswise into coins, plus one 2-inch piece fresh ginger, peeled and julienned

1 bunch cilantro

2 tablespoons sake

2 tablespoons macadamia nut oil

2 cups steamed rice, for serving

Serves 2 to 4

ON THE MENU:

Namasu, page 68

Side salad with Creamy Asian Dressing, page 217

Guava Cake, page 189

Moi, or Pacific threadfin, was once considered the fish of royalty, and centuries ago, only royalty were allowed to eat it. Nowadays, it's still thought of as a delicacy. Flaky and mild flavored, this white-fleshed, silver-and-black-striped fish is an island favorite. Steaming it Chinese-style is a great way to serve it. If you can't find Moi, look for a mild, white-fleshed fish.

In a small bowl, whisk together the sesame oil, soy sauce, sugar, and chili pepper (if using). Set aside.

Using a paring knife, cut three or four 1-inch slits on each side of the fish through the skin to the bone. Pat the fish dry with paper towels and generously season the fish, inside and out, with salt and black pepper. Insert 1 piece of green onion and 1 coin of ginger into each slit and stuff the fish with half of the remaining ginger coins, one-third of the remaining green onions, and one-third of the cilantro. Lay out half the remaining cilantro, the rest of the ginger coins, and half the remaining green onions on the bottom of a steamer basket to create a bed for the fish to rest on. Chop the remaining cilantro leaves and stems and set aside. Place the fish on the bed of aromatics.

In a large pot with the lid on, bring 2 inches of water to boil over high heat. Set the steamer basket in the pot and turn the heat to low, keeping the water at a simmer. Pour the sake over the fish and immediately cover the pot with the lid. Steam until the flesh is opaque and easily flakes, 16 to 20 minutes. Remove the aromatics from the fish and discard. Place the fish on a platter.

In a small saucepan, heat the macadamia nut oil over high heat just until it starts to sizzle. Pour it all over the fish. Add the soy sauce mixture to the saucepan and heat over high heat until hot, less than 1 minute. Pour the sauce over the fish and top with the remaining green onions, chopped cilantro, and julienned ginger. Serve with bowls of steamed rice.

SQUID LŪʻAU

2 pounds taro (lūʻau or kalo) leaves

1¼ cups Hawaiian salt (ʻalaea)

One 1½- to 2-pound octopus

Two or three 12-ounce cans light beer

1½ cups coconut milk

1 tablespoon sugar, or more to taste

Serves 6 to 8

ON THE MENU:

Lomi Salmon, page 59
Poi, page 65
Chicken Long Rice, page 56

This classic Hawaiian dish is the reason why today we call a celebration, or pāʻina, a lūʻau. Since it was served at so many events, the name became synonymous with the parties. Making this stew of lūʻau (taro or kalo) leaves, tender octopus (called heʻe in Hawaiian and tako in Japanese), and creamy coconut milk requires some patience, but the sweet and savory end result is well worth it. And don't be fooled by what the recipe is called, squid lūʻau: octopus is typically used despite the name.

Wearing disposable gloves (see Note, page 65), wash the taro leaves and use a paring knife to remove the stem and any tough veins. Chop the leaves into 3 by 3-inch pieces. Set aside.

Bring a large pot of water to a boil over high heat and add the chopped taro leaves. Turn the heat to medium-low and simmer for about 3 hours, stirring the leaves in a J motion every 10 to 15 minutes to ensure they cook evenly and to avoid burning them on the pot bottom. Add more water as needed.

Meanwhile, add about 1 cup of the salt to the bottom of a large bowl. Stuff the beak (the mouth) of the octopus with the salt. Holding the head, lift the octopus up and down continuously in the salt until the eyes "cry" with black ink, 15 to 20 minutes, then rinse well.

Select a pot that is just big enough for the octopus to fill almost completely. Place the octopus in the pot and add enough of the beer to just cover it. Bring to a boil over high heat, then turn the heat to low and simmer until very tender, about 1½ hours.

Again wearing gloves, remove the octopus from the pot and use your fingers to rub and strip the dark skin away from the meat. Note that cleaning the octopus in this way is easiest while it is still hot. Most of the suckers will be removed at this time, leaving you with clean, white octopus meat. Cut the head away and discard, then cut the meat from the tentacles into ½-inch pieces and set it aside in a bowl.

When the taro leaves are cooked, drain the water from the pot and add ½ cup water, the coconut milk, 1 teaspoon salt, and the sugar. Cook over medium heat, stirring often, for about 15 minutes. Add the reserved octopus and stir until well incorporated. Adjust the salt and sugar to taste. Serve in bowls.

FRIED REEF FISH

6 small reef fish (such as menpachi, manini, or aholehole), cleaned

Kosher salt and freshly ground black pepper

1 cup all-purpose flour

Neutral oil, for frying

Soy sauce (shoyu), for serving

Lemon wedges, for serving

Serves 4

ON THE MENU:

Pohole Fern Salad, page 62
Poi, page 65
Haupia, page 168

True story: I never took to fishing because one of the first and only times I ever went, I caught a stick fish. You might not think it sounds very traumatizing, but tell that to an eight-year-old who didn't realize she caught a stick fish, not a stick, until it jumped out at her! While I wouldn't recommend frying stick fish, I would definitely recommend frying small reef fish, like menpachi. Usually done outside in a wok or skillet set on a propane burner, this simple fried fish is a winner every time. If possible, I'd recommend doing this outside, to avoid filling your home with the smell of fried fish!

Line a plate with paper towels and set aside. On each side of the fish, cut three or four slits through the skin to the bone. Pat the fish dry with paper towels and generously season the fish with salt and pepper. Place the flour in a shallow bowl or dish and coat the fish, on both sides, with flour, dusting off any excess. In a large skillet or a wok, add an inch or two of oil and heat over medium heat to about 350°F. Place the fish in the skillet and fry on both sides for about 3 minutes on each side, until brown and crisp. Drain on the paper towel–lined plate and serve with soy sauce and lemon wedges.

LOCAL-STYLE FISH

4 large ti leaves, tough stems removed

One whole 2-pound Hawaiian pink snapper (opakapaka) or similar fish, cleaned

1 tablespoon Hawaiian salt ('alaea)

1 tablespoon freshly ground black pepper

1½ cups Best Foods (or Hellmann's) mayonnaise

4 garlic cloves, peeled and finely grated

One 1-inch piece fresh ginger, peeled and grated

½ Maui or yellow onion, peeled and sliced

3 vine-ripened tomatoes, sliced

4 green onions, green parts only, chopped

One 5-ounce Portuguese sausage, thinly sliced, or 5 ounces cooked Portuguese Sausage Patties (page 73), broken into pieces

1 cup steamed rice, for serving

Serves 2 to 4

ON THE MENU:

Namasu, page 68

Side salad with Creamy Asian Dressing, page 217

Liliko'i Chiffon Pie, page 159

Stuffed with a mixture of mayonnaise, Portuguese sausage, aromatics, and tomatoes, opakapaka fish is a local favorite. Look for a small snapper (pink or gray) for making this dish.

Preheat the oven to 375°F. Line a rimmed baking sheet with a row of the ti leaves and set it aside.

Using a paring knife, cut three or four 1-inch slits on each side of the fish through the skin to the bone. Pat the fish dry with paper towels and generously season the fish, inside and out, with the salt and black pepper. Coat each side of the fish with ¼ cup of the mayonnaise (½ cup total). In a bowl, combine the remaining 1 cup mayonnaise, the garlic, ginger, Maui onion, tomatoes, green onions, and Portuguese sausage. Stuff the fish with this mixture and place it on the ti leaves. Wrap the ti leaves around the fish and tie with kitchen string or ti leaf strips. Cover the pan with aluminum foil.

Bake the fish until the flesh is opaque and flakes easily, 40 to 50 minutes. Serve with steamed rice.

GINGER MISOYAKI BUTTERFISH

¾ cup white miso paste

¾ cup packed brown sugar

1 cup sake

1 cup mirin

½ cup rice vinegar

¼ cup soy sauce (shoyu)

One ½-inch piece fresh ginger, peeled and finely grated

Four 4-ounce North Pacific sablefish fillets

2 cups steamed rice, for serving

Furikake (see page 31), for serving

Blanched baby bok choy, for serving

Serves 4

ON THE MENU:

Takuan, page 69

Side salad with Guava Dressing, page 219

Macadamia Nut Cream Pie, page 164

Things you learn when you move away from Hawai'i: Butterfish is not a type of fish. It refers to a style of preparation, not an actual fish. What's more confusing is that the type of fish typically used in butterfish dishes is often called black cod, but that fish is actually a North Pacific sablefish! Learn from my mistakes and ask your local fishmonger for North Pacific sablefish fillets when preparing this dish. And plan ahead. While most local grocery stores sell marinated butterfish fillets, it takes 2 to 3 days to marinate your own at home.

In a small saucepan, whisk together the miso paste, brown sugar, sake, mirin, rice vinegar, soy sauce, and ginger. Bring to a simmer over medium heat, whisking occasionally. Turn the heat to low and simmer until the mixture has thickened and reduced by a quarter or so, 45 minutes to 1 hour. Let cool completely.

Place the fillets in a gallon-size ziplock bag and pour the cooled sauce over them. Seal and transfer the bag to the fridge to marinate for 2 to 3 days, turning the bag every 24 hours.

Remove the bag from the refrigerator and let it sit at room temperature for 30 minutes.

Preheat the broiler and raise your oven rack to the top spot; it should be 6 to 8 inches from the coils. Line a rimmed baking sheet with aluminum foil, dull side up.

Wipe off any excess sauce from the top of the fillets and arrange them, skin side down, on the foil-lined baking sheet. Broil until the fish flesh is almost opaque, 8 to 10 minutes. Broil for a minute or two to caramelize the top of the fish; it's done when the outer edges start to blacken. Serve with steamed rice, furikake, and baby bok choy.

NOODLES

(Nulu)

When it comes to carbs, rice may be the reigning champ in Hawai'i, but noodles come in a close second. From Saimin (page 143) to Pansit (page 155), we find lots of ways to eat a variety of noodles. Dry Mein (page 147), a dish that uses saimin noodles, is great for potlucks, as is Somen Salad (page 151). Whether you're craving something soupy, stir-fried, or cold, we've got you covered.

SAIMIN

Noodles
1 tablespoon baking soda

2 teaspoons kosher salt

2 cups cool water

3 large eggs, lightly beaten

3½ cups bread flour

3½ cups cake flour

1 cup cornstarch

Dashi Broth
5 quarts water

One 1½-pound smoked ham hock or shank

1 pound chicken drumsticks or wings

1 ounce dried shrimp (opae; I buy Family Food Company's from Marukai Market)

6 dried shiitake mushrooms, rinsed

5 or 6 green onions

1 teaspoon Hawaiian salt ('alaea)

One 4-inch piece kombu, wiped clean with a wet paper towel

1 tablespoon soy sauce (shoyu)

2 tablespoons mirin

Recommended Garnishes
Char Siu Pork (page 86), julienned

Fish cake (kamaboko), sliced (see Note)

Chopped green onions

Spam, julienned

Thin strips of fried egg omelet (see page 42)

Bean sprouts

Chopped napa cabbage (won bok)

Boiled wontons

Serves 8

Most people take one look at saimin and assume it's Japanese. After all, it sure does look like ramen. But if you look closer, you'll notice a light, clear broth rather than the heavy, thick broth you find in most ramen joints. And then there are the toppings. They look the same, but also different. Ramen is usually topped with some mix of chashu (roasted pork), menma (seasoned bamboo shoot), tamago (usually a soft-boiled shoyu egg), bean sprouts, negi (green onion), kamaboko (fish cake), and even canned corn, whereas saimin is typically topped with a combination of char siu, egg omelet strips, bean sprouts, green onion, kamaboko, chopped won bok (napa cabbage), and boiled wontons. Saimin noodles are made with egg, like fresh chow mein noodles. According to food historians, saimin has Chinese roots, as does, coincidentally, ramen! Sai mihn (Cantonese for "thin noodle") looks pretty Chinese to me, but you be the judge.

My favorite saimin noodles come from Iwamoto Natto Factory in Pā'iu, Maui. They make the noodles for Sam Sato's, a local favorite for dishes like saimin and their famed dry mein (see page 147). While you don't need to make your own, I've included a recipe for them in case you don't have access to fresh noodles. It's worth noting that a pasta machine with a spaghetti cutter is required to make them. If you're on the West or East Coast, look for Sun Noodle brand.

To make the noodles, begin by preheating the oven to 250°F. Line a small rimmed baking sheet with aluminum foil and spread the baking soda on it in a thin, even layer. Bake for 1 hour and let cool completely before using. Be careful not to touch the baked baking soda because, once baked, it becomes more alkaline and can irritate your skin.

Once the baking soda is cool, whisk it in a bowl with the kosher salt and cool water, stirring until the baking soda is dissolved. Next, whisk the eggs into the mixture. Combine both flours in the bowl of a stand mixer fitted with the paddle attachment. Turn the mixer to low speed and, working in four equal additions, slowly pour in the baking soda mixture in a steady stream. Be sure to let the mixer run a little before the next addition. Halfway through, when the dough starts to come together, replace the paddle attachment with the dough hook and knead at medium-low speed until the dough becomes a rough but mostly formed ball, 8 to 10 minutes. Be sure to scrape down the sides at times, if necessary. (If at any point it seems like your mixer is working too hard, turn the dough out and knead by hand.) When the dough is a roughly formed ball, turn it out onto the counter and knead it into a smooth ball. Return it to the bowl and cover with a clean, damp kitchen towel. Let it rest at room temperature for 1 hour.

Press the ball of dough down into a disk and cut it into sixteen equal-size pieces. Return all but one piece to the bowl and re-cover the bowl with

▶▶▶ Continued

ON THE MENU:

the damp kitchen towel (re-dampening it if necessary). Either roll the piece out with a rolling pin, or flatten and work it in the palm of your hand until it's about ¼ inch thick and somewhat rectangular. Run the flattened piece through a pasta machine at the widest setting. Do this three times total, then fold the piece into thirds, like a letter. Flatten the "letter" with the rolling pin or your hands again until it's ¼ inch thick. Run the "letter," seam side on the left, through the pasta machine three times total. Repeat the rolling and folding process two more times, or until the dough is smooth and elastic. Now, turn the dial of your pasta machine one click to a narrower setting and run the dough through three times (you will not be folding anymore). Turn the dial one more click and run the dough through three more times. Repeat this until the dough is ¹⁄₁₆ inch thick. Cut the sheet of dough into foot-long sheets, coat both sides of each sheet with a generous dusting of the cornstarch, and stack on a rimmed baking sheet. Cover the sheets of dough with a clean kitchen towel. Repeat with the remaining pieces of dough.

Fit the pasta machine with the spaghetti cutter and run each dough sheet through the cutter. Cover the cut noodles with the clean kitchen towel until they are all cut, then divide them into eight equal portions and set aside. If not cooking immediately, package the eight servings and refrigerate or freeze for later use. The noodles will keep in an airtight container for 3 days in the refrigerator or 1 month in the freezer.

To prepare the dashi broth, in a large stockpot, combine the water with the ham hock, chicken drumsticks, dried shrimp, shiitake mushrooms, green onions, salt, and kombu. Bring to a boil over high heat. As soon as the mixture is boiling, remove the kombu. Turn the heat to medium and simmer for 2 hours. Strain the broth through a large fine-mesh sieve into another large stockpot. Reserve the chicken and ham hock for another purpose, if you'd like. Place the strained broth over medium-low heat and add the soy sauce and mirin. Simmer for 15 to 20 minutes.

Bring a large pot of water to a boil; if desired, for a clearer broth, bring a second large pot of water to a boil. If you have a noodle basket, place one serving of noodles in it and give a quick rinse under the kitchen faucet to remove any excess cornstarch. Boil the noodles, in the basket, until they rise to the surface, 1 to 3 minutes. Fresh noodles should be done in about a minute; older or frozen noodles will take longer. If using two pots, drain the noodles and move them to the other pot of boiling water for a quick rinse.

Place the noodles in a bowl and ladle the broth over. Serve the noodles with any of the recommended garnishes.

Note: Kamaboko (fish cake) is a processed seafood product usually sold as a semicylindrical white-and-bright-pink loaf. You can find it in the refrigerated section at most markets in Hawai'i or at Japanese markets such as Marukai or Nijiya on the mainland.

DRY MEIN

1½ pounds fresh saimin noodles, homemade (see page 143) or store-bought (such as Iwamoto or Sun Noodle brand)

6 ounces bean sprouts

¼ cup neutral oil

¼ cup soy sauce (shoyu)

2 tablespoons oyster sauce

Freshly ground black pepper

1 pound Char Siu Pork (page 86), julienned

6 green onions, green parts only, chopped

1 recipe dashi broth (see page 143; optional)

4 to 6 Teriyaki Beef Sticks (page 119; optional)

Hot mustard paste (see page 41; optional), for serving

Serves 4 to 6

ON THE MENU:

Local-Style BBQ Chicken, page 108

Teriyaki Beef Sticks, page 119

Pie Crust Manju, page 179

Dry mein is a dry noodle dish made from the same noodles you use in Saimin. It was created by a Chinese cook at the Japanese-owned Sam Sato's restaurant, back when the restaurant was in its first location in Pu'unene. Today, there is almost always a wait during the lunch hour, with locals lining up for their dry mein. The seasoned noodles are topped with julienned char siu pork, chopped green onions, and bean sprouts and served with a side of dashi for dipping, sipping, or pouring all over. My go-to order at the restaurant is one small bowl dry mein, with a side of hot mustard, one barbecued teriyaki beef stick, and one red bean (azuki/adzuki) pie crust manju.

Bring a large pot of water to boil over high heat. Rinse the noodles under the kitchen faucet to remove any excess cornstarch. Place the bean sprouts in a large colander and set in the kitchen sink. Cook the noodles in the boiling water until they begin to float to the top, about 1 minute. Do not overcook the noodles; you want them to be al dente.

Pour the noodles into the colander with the bean sprouts. Give the colander a good shake and transfer the noodles and bean sprouts to a bowl. Toss them with the oil, soy sauce, oyster sauce, and black pepper to taste. Toss in the char siu and green onions. If desired, serve with a bowl of dashi, a teriyaki beef stick, and a small dash of hot mustard.

CHOW FUN

This traditional Cantonese dish is an island favorite. It's served all around town, though my favorite still remains Wailuku Hongwanji Mission's chow fun at the Maui County fair. This is a great weeknight dinner, as it's loaded with veggies and flavors, and it doesn't get much easier than stir-fried noodles.

2 tablespoons neutral oil

3 celery stalks, thinly sliced on the bias

2 carrots, peeled and julienned

1 small Maui or yellow onion, peeled and thinly sliced

Kosher salt and freshly ground black pepper

2 garlic cloves, peeled and minced

6 ounces snow peas, ends trimmed, julienned

6 ounces bean sprouts

12 ounces Char Siu Pork (page 86), julienned

4 green onions, green parts only, cut into 1- to 2-inch pieces

1 pound fresh chow fun noodles, or one 7-ounce package dried chow fun noodles, cooked until al dente

2½ tablespoons oyster sauce

2½ tablespoons soy sauce (shoyu)

Serves 4 to 6

In a large wok or wide skillet, heat 1½ tablespoons of the oil over medium heat until shiny and shimmering. Add the celery, carrots, and Maui onion, season with salt and pepper to taste, and stir-fry until the vegetables are tender, 6 to 8 minutes. Remove the veggies from the pan and set them aside.

Add the remaining ½ tablespoon oil to the pan and stir-fry the garlic, snow peas, bean sprouts, and char siu, seasoning with salt and pepper to taste, for 2 to 3 minutes, until the vegetables are tender. Remove from the pan and set aside with the other stir-fried veggies. Add the green onions and noodles to the pan and toss with the oyster sauce and soy sauce. Add all the reserved stir-fried items back to the pan and toss together, adjusting the seasoning as needed. Serve warm.

ON THE MENU:

Shoyu Chicken, page 103

Side salad with Papaya Seed Dressing, page 218

Butter Mochi, page 167

SOMEN SALAD

Dressing

¼ cup sugar

1 cup low-sodium chicken broth

¼ cup soy sauce (shoyu)

2 tablespoons sesame oil

¼ cup mirin

Salad

½ head napa cabbage (won bok), shredded

1 handful watercress, leaves and stems, coarsely chopped

One 12-ounce package somen noodles (3 bundles), cooked, rinsed with cold water, and drained

8 ounces Char Siu Pork (page 86), julienned

4 ounces fish cake (kamaboko; see Note, page 144), julienned

1 Japanese cucumber or ½ English cucumber, julienned

2 carrots, peeled and julienned

1 handful snow peas, julienned

2 large eggs, beaten, fried into thin omelets, and thinly sliced (see page 42)

3 green onions, green parts only, thinly sliced

Serves 6

ON THE MENU:

Takuan, page 69
Mochiko Chicken, page 100
Kūlolo Bars, page 176

When I was younger, the best part about school was the field trips. It wasn't just a day of freedom from the classroom that I looked forward to; field trips meant we brought our lunch from home, and my mom always packed the best lunches. When she had time, there were homemade Mochiko Chicken (page 100) or Teriyaki Beef Sticks (page 119) and musubi (salted rice balls wrapped in nori), always with a pouch of Capri Sun. When she didn't have time, we'd grab a somen salad from Pukalani Superette. Whenever I make this salad, I pack it up in a to-go container and take it with me to the park or the beach. While I may not be drinking Capri Suns anymore, I still look forward to field trips and somen salad.

To make the dressing, combine the sugar, chicken broth, soy sauce, sesame oil, and mirin in a jar with a lid. Shake together until the sugar has dissolved. Store in the refrigerator until ready to use up to 2 weeks.

To prepare the salad, evenly distribute the cabbage and watercress into the bottom of your serving pan. Cover with the somen noodles. Top with the char siu, fish cake, cucumber, carrots, snow peas, egg strips, and green onions.

When you are ready to serve, simply pour on the dressing and toss.

CHICKEN HEKKA

1 tablespoon neutral oil

1 pound boneless, skinless chicken thighs, cut into 1-inch wide strips

One 1-inch piece fresh ginger, peeled and grated

2 garlic cloves, peeled and finely grated

½ cup soy sauce (shoyu)

½ cup mirin

¼ cup packed brown sugar

1 tablespoon sesame oil

3 cups chicken broth

2 carrots, peeled and julienned

½ Maui or yellow onion, peeled and sliced

3½ ounces brown beech mushrooms (bunashimeji), trimmed and each cluster separated into individual mushrooms

One 8-ounce can sliced bamboo shoots in water, drained

One 5.3-ounce package bean thread noodles, soaked in hot water for 30 minutes, drained, and cut in half

1 bunch green onions, white and green parts, cut into 1- to 2-inch pieces

1 bunch watercress, stems trimmed

Serves 4 to 6

ON THE MENU:

Lumpia, page 48

Side salad with Liliko'i Vinaigrette, page 218

Cascaron, page 180

This is a clean-out-the-fridge kind of dish, which is why my mom made it a lot when I was growing up. It's the local version of Japanese sukiyaki. You can add just about any vegetable you want—celery, carrots, bean sprouts, green onion, or canned bamboo shoots. I personally love it with buttery, nutty beech mushrooms, which come in clusters and are usually packaged. If you can't find them, feel free to substitute sliced cremini mushrooms. Cooked in an easy-to-make broth, this makes for a hearty and healthy meal. It's a dish that my grandma made for my mom, and my great-grandma made for my grandma. And now I make it for my boyfriend.

In a large skillet or wok, heat the neutral oil over medium heat until shiny and shimmering. Add the chicken and cook until it is browned and cooked through, 4 to 5 minutes. Add the ginger and garlic and cook for a minute. Add the soy sauce, mirin, brown sugar, sesame oil, and chicken broth and bring to a boil over medium-high heat.

Turn the heat to low and simmer for 10 to 15 minutes. Add the carrots, Maui onion, mushrooms, and bamboo shoots and simmer until the vegetables are tender, about 5 minutes. Add the bean thread noodles and green onions and cook for 2 to 3 minutes. Remove from the heat and serve in bowls, topped with the watercress.

PANSIT

4 ounces rice stick noodles (pancit bihon)

3 dried shiitake mushrooms

Boiling water, for soaking

1 tablespoon neutral oil

8 ounces lean pork, thinly sliced

Kosher salt and freshly ground black pepper

4 garlic cloves, peeled and minced

3 carrots, peeled and julienned

3 celery stalks, julienned

½ Maui or yellow onion, peeled and sliced

8 ounces small (51/60) raw shrimp, peeled and deveined

1 cup chicken broth

4 ounces pancit canton or saimin

3 tablespoons soy sauce (shoyu)

2 teaspoons fish sauce

¼ teaspoon freshly ground black pepper

¼ head napa cabbage (won bok), shredded

Calamansi halves or lemon wedges, for serving

Serves 4 to 6

ON THE MENU:

Lumpia, page 48

Side salad with Payaya Seed Dressing, page 218

Butter Mochi, page 167

Pansit (or pancit) is traditionally made with pancit bihon, a rice stick noodle; pancit canton, a wheat-flour stick noodle; or a combination of the two. In Hawai'i, it's not uncommon to find it made with bean thread noodles and/or saimin noodles. If you can't find pancit canton or saimin noodles, feel free to double the amount of rice stick noodles. It's great served with a squeeze of calamansi, a Filipino citrus with bright orange flesh, but if you can't find calamansi, lemon works too!

Place the rice stick noodles and mushrooms in a bowl and cover them with boiling water. Soak for 10 minutes, then drain the water. Cut the noodles in half and slice the shiitake, removing and discarding the stems. Set aside.

In a large wok or wide skillet, heat the oil over medium heat until shiny and shimmering. Season the pork with salt and pepper, add it to the skillet, and sauté until it is cooked through and browned, 4 to 5 minutes. Remove the pork from the pan and add the garlic, carrots, celery, and onion and sauté until tender, about 5 minutes. Add the shrimp and sauté for 1 minute more.

Set a pot over medium-high heat, add the chicken broth, and bring it to a boil. Turn the heat to medium-low and add the pancit canton. Simmer for 2 minutes, then add the rice stick noodles and simmer for 2 minutes more. Drain the noodles into a colander and add them to the wok along with the reserved pork and shiitake mushrooms. Add the soy sauce and fish sauce and gently toss everything together with tongs. Add the cabbage and pepper and simmer for 2 minutes more. Serve warm with calamansi halves.

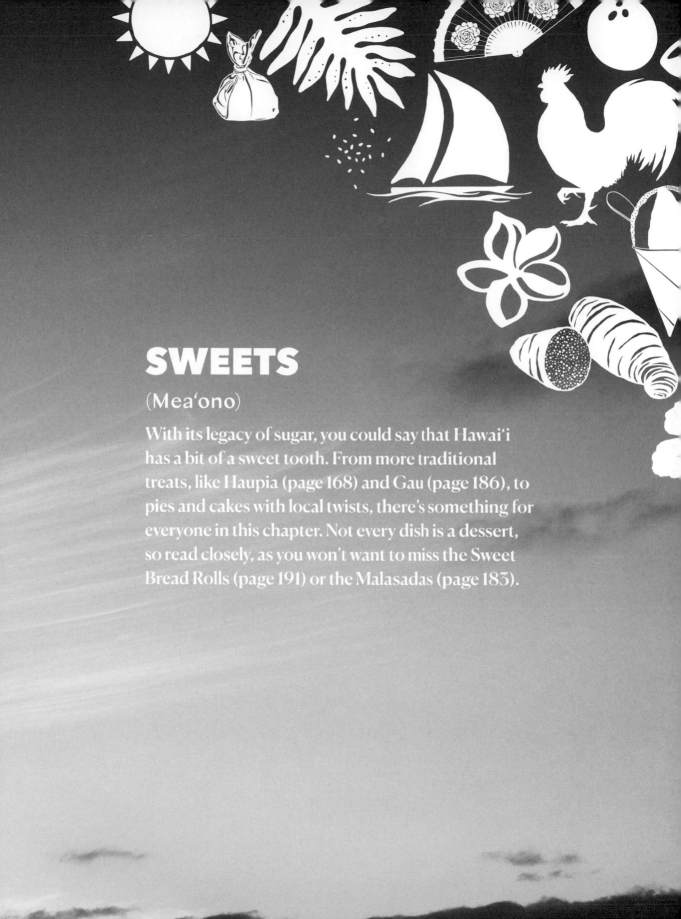

SWEETS

(Mea'ono)

With its legacy of sugar, you could say that Hawai'i
has a bit of a sweet tooth. From more traditional
treats, like Haupia (page 168) and Gau (page 186), to
pies and cakes with local twists, there's something for
everyone in this chapter. Not every dish is a dessert,
so read closely, as you won't want to miss the Sweet
Bread Rolls (page 191) or the Malasadas (page 183).

LILIKOʻI CHIFFON PIE

Pie Crust
1¼ cups all-purpose flour
½ teaspoon kosher salt
2 teaspoons granulated sugar
1 teaspoon apple cider vinegar
⅓ cup ice-cold water
½ cup cold unsalted butter, cut into ½-inch cubes
1 large egg white beaten with 1 teaspoon water

Liliko'i Chiffon
¼ cup ice-cold water
3½ teaspoons unflavored gelatin powder
6 large eggs, separated
1¼ cups liliko'i (passion fruit) pulp
1 cup granulated sugar
½ teaspoon kosher salt

Stabilized Whipped Cream
1 tablespoon ice-cold water
½ teaspoon unflavored gelatin powder
1 cup cold heavy whipping cream
2 teaspoons confectioners' sugar
½ teaspoon vanilla extract

Fresh liliko'i (passion fruit) seeds, for garnish (optional)

Makes one 9-inch pie

If you've ever visited Kaua'i, chances are you've heard of Hamura's Saimin. Located near the airport in Līhu'e, the spot is known for two things: saimin and liliko'i (passion fruit) chiffon pie. The first time I tried the pie, I knew it was a forever memory. From its light-as-air chiffon filling to the fluffy whipped cream on top, this pie is like a liliko'i cloud. It takes a bit of time to make, but it is worth all the effort. If you can't find fresh liliko'i, check the freezer section of your local grocery store. Goya Foods makes a frozen 100 percent passion fruit pulp, and it is just as good as homemade. If you can't find Goya, try Ceres brand 100 percent passion fruit juice.

To make the crust, whisk the flour, salt, and granulated sugar together in a bowl. Whisk the vinegar into the cold water and set it aside. Toss the butter in the flour mixture and use a pastry blender or your fingers to evenly blend it into the flour until the pieces are pea size. If the mixture begins to get too warm and the butter feels soft, simply pop the bowl into the freezer for a few minutes. Next, drizzle 3 tablespoons of the cold water over the mixture. Stir in the water with a rubber spatula and add additional water, a teaspoon at a time, until you can squeeze a chunk together without it falling apart; it should look shaggy. Use your hands to press the dough together to form a ball, then flatten the ball into a disk. Wrap the dough in plastic wrap and chill in the refrigerator for 1 hour before using.

Preheat the oven to 425°F.

On a lightly floured clean work surface, roll the dough out into a round about 3 inches wider than the size of your pie dish (I recommend a 9-inch dish); the dough should be about ⅛ inch thick. Gently fold the round in half and carefully transfer it to the dish. Unfold the round and trim it so there's about 1 inch of excess dough hanging over. Fold that excess dough under itself and crimp the edges. Using a fork, pierce the dough ten to fifteen times, all around the bottom and a few times on the sides. This will allow the dough to release steam as it bakes. Transfer the dish to the freezer to chill until very firm, about 15 minutes.

Remove the dough from the freezer, completely cover it with aluminum foil, and fill with pie weights. Bake for 20 minutes. Gently and carefully remove the foil and pie weights and lower the oven temperature to 375°F. Use a pastry brush to brush the crust all over with the beaten egg white and water. Return the crust to the oven and bake until golden brown, 8 to 10 minutes. Remove from the oven and let cool on a rack.

To make the chiffon, prepare an ice-water bath by filling a bowl with water and a handful of ice cubes and set it aside. Put the cold water in a small bowl and evenly sprinkle the gelatin powder over it. Set this bowl aside to let the gelatin bloom (hydrate) while you work on the rest

▶▶▶ Continued

ON THE MENU:

Portuguese Bean Soup, page 97

Sweet Bread Rolls, page 191

Side salad with Guava Dressing, page 219

of the chiffon. Set a double boiler over medium-low heat and bring the water to a simmer. In the top pan or bowl of your double boiler, whisk together the egg yolks, liliko'i pulp, ½ cup of the granulated sugar, and salt. Continue whisking until the mixture has thickened to the consistency of a thin glue, 25 to 30 minutes. Be patient; the mixture will thicken and thin before thickening again. When it coats the back of a wooden spoon, it is thick enough (it will thicken further with the addition of the gelatin). Remove the bowl from the heat and whisk in the gelatin until it has completely dissolved, 2 to 3 minutes. Strain the mixture through a fine-mesh sieve into a bowl, pressing with the back of the wooden spoon. Set the strained mixture over the ice bath to cool quickly.

Meanwhile, set up the double boiler again with a clean top pan or bowl. Combine the egg whites and the remaining ½ cup granulated sugar in the pan or bowl and, using a silicone spatula, stir continuously until the sugar has dissolved completely and the mixture is warm, 2 to 3 minutes.

Pour the mixture into the bowl of a stand mixer fitted with the whisk attachment. Whisk on low speed until frothy, then slowly increase to high and whisk until the mixture is light and fluffy and can hold a stiff peak, a minute or two. You can test this by lifting the whisk attachment up and out of the bowl; if you can invert the bowl and the peak holds, it's done. Be carefully not to overwhip this.

Whisk the cooled liliko'i mixture, breaking up with your whisk any parts that have started to set. Use your spatula to fold in the egg whites in four additions, making sure they are fully incorporated, without any white streaks. Gently pour the chiffon mixture into the cooled baked pie crust. Loosely cover the pie with plastic wrap and transfer to the freezer to set for 1 hour.

To make the whipped cream, put the cold water in a small bowl and evenly sprinkle the gelatin powder over it. Let the gelatin sit and bloom for 5 minutes, then microwave for 5 seconds to dissolve the gelatin. Whisk the mixture to fully dissolve the gelatin, if necessary. Fit the stand mixer with the whisk attachment and combine the cream, confectioners' sugar, and vanilla in the mixer bowl. Whisk the mixture on medium speed until bubbles form, then gradually increase the speed to high. Turn the speed to low and add the gelatin mixture, then gradually turn the speed back up to high. Mix until light and fluffy and soft peaks form, 2 to 3 minutes. Gently spread the whipped cream over the top of the frozen chiffon filling and return the pie to the freezer until ready to serve.

Remove the pie from the freezer and let thaw for 20 to 30 minutes before slicing and serving. If desired, garnish the top of the pie with fresh liliko'i seeds.

DOUBLE-CHOCOLATE HAUPIA PIE

Chocolate Filling

½ cup sugar

½ teaspoon kosher salt

3 tablespoons cornstarch

¼ cup unsweetened Dutch process cocoa powder

2 cups whole milk

4 large egg yolks, beaten

5 ounces semisweet or bittersweet chocolate, finely chopped

2 tablespoons unsalted butter, cut into pieces

1 tablespoon vanilla extract

1 baked and cooled pie crust (see page 159)

Haupia

⅓ cup sugar

Pinch of kosher salt

3 tablespoons cornstarch

1½ cups coconut milk

½ cup whole milk

1 batch stabilized whipped cream (see page 159)

Makes one 9-inch pie

ON THE MENU:

Chicken Adobo, page 107

Dry Mein, page 147

Side salad with Liliko'i Vinaigrette, page 218

Ted's Bakery on the North Shore of O'ahu is famous for its chocolate haupia pie. After a morning beach session, tourists and locals alike flock to the tiny shop for lunch and, of course, pie. My version is extra chocolaty, which, when combined with the light and mellow coconut, makes for a well-balanced yet oh-so-decadant dessert. It is the perfect way to end any meal, in my opinion.

To make the filling, in a medium saucepan, whisk the sugar, salt, cornstarch, and cocoa powder together. Pour the milk into the mixture in a slow, steady stream while you continue to whisk. Cook the mixture over medium heat, whisking continuously, until it comes to a boil, 6 to 8 minutes. Remove from the heat. Whisk about 1 cup of the hot chocolate mixture into the beaten egg yolks until fully incorporated, then add this egg mixture back to the saucepan. Place the mixture over medium-low heat and bring to a simmer, whisking the entire time, until it is thick enough to coat the back of a spoon, 2 to 3 minutes.

Strain the mixture through a fine-mesh sieve into a clean bowl, using a wooden spoon to help push the pudding through. Add the chopped chocolate, butter, and vanilla to the pudding and whisk until the chocolate and butter are melted and fully incorporated, about 2 minutes. The mixture should be smooth. Pour the mixture into the cooled pie crust and cover the surface with a piece of plastic wrap.

To make the haupia, in a saucepan, combine the sugar, salt, and cornstarch. Whisk in the coconut milk and set the pan over medium-high heat. Whisk continuously until the mixture starts to simmer. Immediately turn the heat to medium-low and continue to whisk continuously until the mixture begins to thicken, 4 to 6 minutes. The mixture will go from liquid to very liquid before it starts to thicken, so be patient. Pour in the whole milk in a steady stream while continuing to whisk. Raise the heat to medium and continue whisking until the mixture has thickened to the consistency of a thick glue and coats the back of a spoon, another 4 to 6 minutes. Remove from the heat.

Remove the plastic wrap from the chocolate filling and pour the hot haupia mixture over the chocolate filling. Let it cool for 10 minutes before covering the top of the pie with a sheet of plastic wrap. Transfer the pie to the refrigerator to chill and set for 2 hours before serving.

Top with whipped cream and serve!

MACADAMIA NUT CREAM PIE

¾ cup sugar

2 cups whole milk

6 large egg yolks, lightly beaten

⅓ cup cornstarch

Pinch of kosher salt

1 tablespoon unsalted butter

2 teaspoons vanilla extract

½ cup plus 2 tablespoons chopped, toasted, salted, dry-roasted macadamia nuts

1 baked and cooled pie crust (see page 159)

2 batches stabilized whipped cream (see page 159)

Makes one 9-inch pie

ON THE MENU:

Namasu, page 68

Ginger Misoyaki Butterfish, page 139

Side salad with Guava Dressing, page 219

When I was younger, my Aunty Sandy and Uncle Bob had a macadamia nut farm. They grew and roasted the best mac nuts I've ever had, and I never appreciated how great the nuts were until the day they sold the farm. Rich and buttery, macadamia nuts add a nice crunch and subtle sweetness to this pie. Fun fact: To correct a common misconception, macadamia nuts are actually indigenous to Australia, not Hawai'i.

In a saucepan, combine ¼ cup of the sugar and the milk. Heat over medium heat for 2 to 3 minutes, until the mixture begins to steam, then immediately remove the pan from the heat. Meanwhile, in a bowl, whisk the remaining ½ cup sugar, egg yolks, cornstarch, and salt together until smooth. Slowly ladle about 1 cup of the hot milk mixture, ¼ cup at a time, into the egg yolks, whisking the entire time. Pour the tempered yolk mixture into the saucepan and cook, whisking continuously, until thick, 5 to 6 minutes. Remove the saucepan from the heat and whisk in the butter and vanilla until smooth. Stir in ½ cup of the macadamia nuts.

Pour the filling into the cooled pie crust and cover with a piece of plastic wrap directly touching the surface of the filling. Let cool to room temperature, then transfer the pie to the refrigerator to chill and set for 2 hours before serving.

Remove from the plastic wrap, top with the whipped cream and the remaining chopped macadamia nuts, and serve!

BUTTER MOCHI

4 large eggs

2 teaspoons vanilla extract

2 cups skim milk

One 1-pound box mochiko flour (see page 28)

2 cups sugar

2 teaspoons baking powder

½ teaspoon kosher salt

½ cup unsalted butter, melted

One 13½-ounce can coconut milk

½ cup unsweetened shredded coconut

A few pinches of flaky salt (optional)

Makes 20 pieces

ON THE MENU:

Mac Salad, page 55

Loco Moco, page 115

Side salad with Papaya Seed Dressing, page 218

Butter mochi is a mainstay at any island party. You can see why: it's like a perfectly chewy, slightly sticky, and just-dense-enough coconut-custard glutinous rice cake. What I love about it is how it evolves over the course of twenty-four hours. The first day it's got this gorgeous, golden brown, crispy, crunchy crust that magically transforms into a soft, almost melty crust the next day. While you can halve the recipe, I doubt you'll want to after trying a bite!

Preheat the oven to 350°F. Grease a 9 by 13-inch baking pan with butter or oil.

In a bowl, whisk together the eggs, vanilla, and milk. In another larger bowl, whisk together the mochiko, sugar, baking powder, and kosher salt. Pour the wet ingredients into the dry ingredients and, with a wooden spoon, stir until well combined. Add the melted butter and coconut milk and mix until fully incorporated. Pour the mixture into the prepared pan and rap the pan on the counter a couple of times to bring any air bubbles up to the surface. Evenly sprinkle the shredded coconut on top of the mixture, a handful at a time, being careful not to jiggle the pan too much, as you want the coconut to stay on the top. Then sprinkle on a few pinches of flaky salt, if desired.

Bake until the mochi is set and golden brown on top, about 1 hour. Set the pan on a wire rack and let cool completely before slicing into rectangles using a plastic knife to minimize sticking; I cut four columns and five rows to make twenty 2¼ by 2½-inch pieces. If the knife seems to be sticking, rub it with a little unsalted butter or neutral oil. Store in an airtight container at room temperature for up to 3 days.

HAUPIA

⅔ cup sugar

¼ teaspoon kosher salt

½ cup cornstarch

3 cups coconut milk

1⅓ cups whole milk

Toasted coconut flakes, for garnish (optional)

Makes 25 squares

ON THE MENU:

Poi, page 65

Pohole Fern Salad, page 62

Squid Lū'au, page 134

Found at lū'au, potlucks, and other events, haupia is a classic Hawaiian dessert. While it is commonly known as a coconut pudding, the texture is similar to a panna cotta—not quite as dense as Jell-O but not as soft as a traditional pudding. Made with a few simple ingredients, it's always a crowd-pleaser. Use the best coconut you can find. Serve this chilled at the end of a meal.

In a medium saucepan, combine the sugar, salt, and cornstarch. Whisk in the coconut milk and set over medium-high heat. Whisk continuously until the mixture starts to simmer. Immediately turn the heat to medium-low and continue to whisk continuously until the mixture begins to thicken, 4 to 6 minutes. The mixture will go from liquid to very liquid before it starts to thicken.

Pour in the whole milk in a steady stream while continuing to whisk. Bring the heat back up to medium and continue whisking until the mixture has thickened to the consistency of a thick glue and can coat the back of a spoon, another 4 to 6 minutes.

Remove from the heat, pour into an 8-inch square baking pan, and smooth the top with a rubber spatula. Let cool for 10 minutes before covering the top of the pan with a sheet of plastic wrap. Transfer the pan to the refrigerator to chill and set for 2 hours. For an extra-smooth top, carefully place a sheet of plastic wrap directly on the top of the haupia after it has cooled for 10 minutes.

Remove the plastic wrap and, using a sharp knife, cut five columns and five rows to make 25 squares. Place each piece in a paper muffin-tin liner and serve chilled. If desired, sprinkle the toasted coconut flakes on top, right before serving.

SWEET POTATO HAUPIA BARS

2 pounds Okinawan sweet potatoes

2 cups all-purpose flour

½ cup sugar

1 cup cold unsalted butter, cut into ½-inch cubes

¾ cup salted dry-roasted macadamia nuts, coarsely chopped

½ cup unsalted butter, at room temperature

¾ cup sugar

2 large eggs

½ cup whole milk

1 teaspoon vanilla extract

¼ teaspoon kosher salt

1 batch Haupia (page 168), before serving

Makes 28 bars

ON THE MENU:

Namasu, page 68

Spam Fried Rice, page 89

Mochiko Chicken, page 100

A twist on the classic Hawaiian treat, these bars are as tasty as they are beautiful. The contrasting layers differ not only in color but in texture. Not too sweet, these bars are well balanced and appeal to even the pickiest eater.

Preheat the oven to 350°F and line a baking sheet with parchment paper. Everything will be baked at this temperature, so keep the oven on throughout. Begin by baking the sweet potatoes. Prick the sweet potatoes all over with a fork, at least five times on each potato. Set them on the prepared baking sheet and bake for 40 minutes to 1 hour, depending on the size of the potatoes. Start checking the doneness after 35 minutes. To check if they are done, simply insert a fork into the middle of the potato; if it goes in easily with little resistance, it's done. Set the baked potatoes on a wire rack to cool. When cool enough to handle, peel off the skins from the potatoes and cut them into 1-inch cubes. Transfer the cubes to the bowl of a stand mixer fitted with the paddle attachment and beat on medium speed for 1 to 2 minutes, until smooth and fluffy. Remove from the bowl, cover, and set aside.

To make the shortbread layer, meanwhile, in a large bowl, combine the flour and ½ cup sugar and give it a quick mix with a wooden spoon or your hands. Using a pastry blender, cut the cold unsalted butter into the flour mixture, blending until the mixture resembles coarse sand. If you don't have a pastry blender, you can combine the sugar and butter in a food processor and pulse until the butter is pea size; add the flour and pulse until it resembles coarse sand. Add the macadamia nuts and mix with a wooden spoon or your hands. Press the mixture into a 9 by 13-inch baking pan and prick with a fork ten to fifteen times all over the surface. Bake until the crust is golden brown, 15 to 20 minutes. Set the pan on a wire rack to cool.

In a large bowl, combine the room-temperature butter and ¾ cup sugar and beat with a hand mixer on medium-low speed. Add the eggs, one at a time, mixing on low to incorporate. Add the sweet potatoes and mix on medium-low until thoroughly combined. Add the milk, vanilla, and salt, mixing on low until well combined. Pour the mixture over the baked crust and bake until the potato has set and has a pale golden tone on top, 30 to 35 minutes. Turn off the oven. Set the pan on a wire rack and let the potato layer cool for 30 minutes before making the haupia layer.

Pour the haupia over the top of the cooled potato layer and let cool for 10 minutes. Cover with plastic wrap and transfer the pan to the refrigerator to chill and set for 2 hours. For an extra-smooth top, carefully place a sheet of plastic wrap directly on the top of the haupia after it has cooled for 10 minutes.

When chilled, slice the bars into rectangles to serve; I usually cut four columns and seven rows to make 28 squares.

SHAVE ICE

Strawberry Syrup

1 pound fresh ripe strawberries, hulled and sliced

1 cup sugar

1½ cups water

2 to 3 drop red food coloring gel (optional)

Liliko'i Syrup

¾ cup liliko'i (passion fruit) pulp (see page 159)

1 cup sugar

1½ cups water

Vanilla Syrup

1½ cups sugar

1¾ cups water

1 vanilla bean, split and scraped

2 to 3 drops blue food coloring gel (optional)

8 to 10 cups ice, for shaving

Vanilla ice cream, for serving (optional)

Li hing powder (see page 30), for sprinkling (optional)

Makes 4 to 6 servings

ON THE MENU:

Takuan, page 69

Beef Curry, page 124

Side salad with Creamy Asian Dressing, page 217

Almost every great beach day ends with a shave ice, a hot-weather treat that is said to have originated from the Japanese kakigōri. Rainbow colored and feathery soft, shave ice is made of finely shaved ice, not crushed ice like is used for snow cones. To make it at home, you will need to purchase a shave ice machine from an Asian market or Amazon. The best shave ice is always made with fresh fruit syrups, but in a pinch, Malolo is a popular brand of premade syrups in Hawai'i.

To make the syrups, place the individual syrup ingredients, except the food coloring, into their own saucepans and bring each to a boil over medium-high heat. Turn the heat to low and simmer for 20 minutes. Let the mixtures cool to room temperature; add the food coloring (if using) and strain the strawberry and passion fruit mixtures through a fine-mesh sieve (not necessary for the vanilla). Transfer each syrup to a separate bottle and chill until ready to use up to 1 month.

Use a shave ice machine to shave the ice. Alternatively, you can process the ice through a food processor, though the shave will not be as fine. Add a scoop of vanilla ice cream to the bottom of a paper cone, if you'd like. Pack shave ice into the cone and drizzle on the syrup. You can also sprinkle on li hing powder, if desired. Serve immediately.

ICE CAKE

1 cup evaporated milk

1 cup water

1 cup Liliko'i Syrup, Strawberry Syrup, or Vanilla Syrup (see page 172)

Makes 8 cups

ON THE MENU:

Maki Sushi, page 42

Potato Mac Salad, page 55

Maui-Style Kalbi Short Ribs, page 120

When I was in middle school, my favorite afternoon treat was an ice cake. A remnant of the plantations, this no-frills sweet is made with only a few ingredients. While it's becoming harder and harder to find in stores, ice cakes are easy to make and are the answer to a hot summer day. Besides the short ingredient list, all you need for these are eight 4-ounce paper cups and small wooden spoons for serving.

Have ready eight 4-ounce paper cups. In a bowl, whisk the evaporated milk, water, and desired syrup together. Pour 6 tablespoons of the mixture into each paper cup. Freeze until frozen solid, at least 3 hours or up to 2 weeks.

Briefly run an upside-down cup under warm water to loosen the ice cake, remove the ice cake and then flip it back over into the cup. Serve immediately with small wooden spoons.

KŪLOLO BARS

1½ pounds cleaned and peeled taro (kalo) root (see Note, page 65), finely grated (about 3 cups)

8 ounces finely grated fresh coconut meat (about 2 cups)

One 13½-ounce can coconut milk

½ cup water

¾ cup packed dark brown sugar

Makes 25 pieces

ON THE MENU:

Lomi Salmon, page 59
Chicken Long Rice, page 56
Pork Laulau, page 78

In its traditional form, kūlolo is thick, coarse, and similar in texture to gummy cooked rice. It's typically steamed for long hours or baked in an imu (earthen oven) overnight. When you're eating it, you're almost certain to find it sticking all over your fingers. While steamed kūlolo is sticky all over, these bars are a twist on the classic Hawaiian confection. They're baked and have a thick yet airy outer crust and a smooth, dense, and gooey center. Not too sweet, these are perfect with an afternoon cup of tea.

Preheat the oven to 350°F. Line a 9-inch square baking pan with two pieces of parchment paper so there's overhang on all sides. Combine the taro, coconut meat and milk, water, and brown sugar in the bowl of a food processor and process until thoroughly combined and very smooth, about 2 minutes. Pour the mixture into the lined pan. Use a spatula to make sure the batter is evenly distributed and smooth on top. Fold over the overhanging paper to encase the mixture, then cover the pan with aluminum foil.

Bake for 2½ hours. Remove the foil and open up the parchment and bake for another 15 minutes. Remove from the oven and let the kūlolo cool completely in the pan.

Using the parchment, lift the cooled kūlolo from the pan. To serve, use a plastic knife (to minimize sticking) to cut five columns and five rows to make 25 squares. If not serving immediately, or for leftovers, wrap the bars tightly with plastic wrap and store in a cool, dry place for up to 2 days.

PIE CRUST MANJU

One 17½-ounce package of azuki (red bean) paste (tsubu an)

2½ cups all-purpose flour

½ teaspoon table salt

2 tablespoons sugar

½ cup plus 2 tablespoons unsalted butter, melted

½ cup water

A few ice cubes

1 teaspoon apple cider vinegar

1 large egg yolk

1 tablespoon whole milk

Makes 12 manju

ON THE MENU:

Pohole Fern Salad, page 62
Mochiko Chicken, page 100
Saimin, page 143

Best served straight from the oven, this Japanese pastry is great with coffee or tea and can be eaten in the morning with your breakfast or in the afternoon as a snack. Filled with either azuki (red bean) paste or lima bean paste, these manju are often boxed up by the dozen and given as omiyage, which is a gift or souvenir you give to your family, friends, or even coworkers after returning from a trip. While there are a few forms for the outer shell, pie crust is by far my favorite.

Preheat the oven to 400°F. Line a baking sheet with parchment paper and set it aside.

Scoop 2 tablespoons of the azuki bean paste and roll it into a ball. (If the filling is too sticky, you can splash a little water on your hands.) Repeat until you have 12 balls. Place them on a plate and cover with plastic wrap to prevent the balls from drying out.

In a bowl, whisk together the flour, salt, and sugar. Pour in the melted butter in a steady stream, mixing it in with a wooden spoon.

In a small bowl, combine the water, ice, and vinegar, swirling it with a spoon to help it chill quickly. Add 7 tablespoons of the ice-water mixture to the flour-butter mixture, stirring with the wooden spoon until it becomes a shaggy mess. When it gets too hard to mix with the spoon, use your hands to mix until just combined. Turn out the dough onto a clean work surface and shape into a disk. Cut the disk into 12 equal pieces, transfer them back to the bowl, and cover with a clean towel to prevent the dough from drying out.

Working with one piece at a time, roll each piece of dough into a ball, then lightly flatten it with your hand to form a disk. Generously flour your work surface and rolling pin and roll the dough, making a quarter turn every time and rolling toward your body with each roll. When the round is 5 inches wide, use the rolling pin to make the outer edges slightly thinner than the rest of the round. This will make it easier to form and seal the edges around the azuki bean filling.

Place 1 ball of filling in the middle of your dough round. Moisten the thin edges of the dough with a wet fingertip. Gather the dough together by pleating the edges of the dough round repeatedly, pinching them together after each pleat until the dough is sealed around the azuki ball. Turn the ball over in your palm, pleat side down, and use the other hand to gently press into a rounded ball with a flat bottom. Set on the prepared baking sheet and repeat until all the dough and filling has been used.

In a small bowl, whisk the egg yolk together with the milk to form an egg wash. Using a pastry brush, glaze the tops of balls with the egg wash. Bake for 20 minutes. Carefully flip all the manju over, seam side up, and return to the oven to bake for another 5 minutes, until golden brown. Transfer to a wire rack, right side up, to cool. Manju will keep at room temperature in an airtight container for 2 to 3 days, but they are best the first day.

CASCARON

One 1-pound box mochiko flour (see page 28)

1½ cups packed brown sugar

2 cups unsweetened shredded coconut

2 cups coconut milk

Neutral oil, for deep-frying

⅓ cup water

Makes about 30 balls

ON THE MENU:

Lumpia, page 48

Mac Salad, page 55

Pork and Peas, page 94

When I was younger, I used to get these sticks at Ka'ahumanu Mall in Kahului, Maui, during the weekly farmers' market. I like to describe cascaron as slightly sweet, coconutty balls of fried mochi. They are easy to make and are best served the day they are made.

In a bowl, whisk together the mochiko, ½ cup of the brown sugar, and the coconut. Mix in the coconut milk, stirring with a wooden spoon until there are no dry clumps. Form into golf ball-size pieces and roll on a clean work surface until round.

Line a rimmed baking sheet with paper towels. Fill a wide Dutch oven or other pot with 2 inches of oil. Heat the pot over medium-low heat to 325°F. Alternatively, a deep fryer can be used. Fry the balls in batches until golden brown and cooked through, 3 to 4 minutes per batch; test for doneness by cutting into a ball. Transfer to the prepared baking sheet to drain. Thread 3 or 4 warm balls onto each bamboo skewer and place the skewers on a wire rack set over a rimmed baking sheet.

Combine the remaining 1 cup brown sugar and the water in a small saucepan and bring to a boil over medium-high heat. Cook until the sugar is completely dissolved, about 1 minute, then pour the sugar mixture all over the balls, turning the skewers as needed. Let cool for 10 minutes before serving warm.

MALASADAS

Dough

¾ cup whole milk, warmed (100° to 110°F)

¾ cup evaporated milk, warmed (100° to 110°F)

3 tablespoons unsalted butter, melted

Two 0.25-ounce packages active dry yeast (4½ teaspoons total)

1 teaspoon sugar, plus ¾ cup and more for dusting

3 large eggs

4 cups bread flour

¾ teaspoon kosher salt

Neutral oil, for deep-frying

Pastry Cream

¾ cup sugar

2 cups whole milk

6 large egg yolks, lightly beaten

¼ cup cornstarch

Pinch of kosher salt

1 tablespoon unsalted butter

1 teaspoon vanilla extract

½ cup liliko'i (passion fruit) juice

Makes 20 to 24 malasadas

ON THE MENU:

Poi, page 65
Pickled Onion, page 67
Local-Style Fish, page 137

Leonard's Bakery in Honolulu, O'ahu, is world famous for its malasadas, Portuguese doughnuts rolled in granulated sugar and usually filled with haupia or macadamia pastry cream. You'll understand why when you bite into these hot, pillowy, sugar-coated doughnuts. While I love going to Leonard's for a freshly fried malasada, I actually prefer making my own. One of my favorite memories is producing them in my Los Angeles kitchen for my friend Lily, who had never had a malasada, and watching her take that first bite. Lily and I both grew up in Maui, about ten minutes from each other, but we didn't meet until we were both living in LA. And while you'd think that we'd share the same food memories from Maui, they couldn't be more different. Lily grew up vegetarian in a Maui-hippie family, where ingredients like spirulina and nutritional yeast were daily staples, while I was raised in a family that made all the local favorites. Vegetarian or not, your first bite of a malasada is one to be treasured.

To make the dough, in a bowl, combine both milks, the butter, yeast, and 1 teaspoon sugar and whisk together. Let the mixture sit until the yeast is activated and foamy, about 10 minutes.

In the bowl of a stand mixer fitted with the paddle attachment, beat the eggs and the remaining ¾ cup sugar together on medium speed for 2 to 3 minutes, until light and fluffy. Turn the speed to low and incorporate the flour and the milk mixture in four additions, alternating between wet and dry ingredients. Add the salt and switch to the dough hook. Gradually turn the speed up to medium-high and knead the dough until it's smooth and pulls away from the sides of the bowl, about 5 minutes. Turn the dough out onto a clean work surface and quickly grease the mixer bowl with butter. Transfer the dough back to the bowl, loosely cover with plastic wrap or a clean kitchen towel, and set it in a warm place to rise until doubled in size, 1 to 2 hours.

Lightly grease a large piece of parchment paper and set it aside. On a lightly floured surface, roll out the dough ½ inch thick. Using a 3-inch biscuit cutter or 3-inch glass bowl, cut out as many rounds as you can, gathering and reusing all the scraps. You should be able to make 20 to 24 rounds. Place them on the greased parchment paper, spacing them 3 inches apart. Cover the rounds with a clean kitchen towel and let rise in a warm place until doubled in size, about 1 hour.

Fill a shallow bowl with some sugar and set aside. Fill a wide Dutch oven or other pot with 2 inches of oil. Heat the pot over medium heat to 350°F. Alternatively, a deep fryer can be used. Using scissors, cut the greased parchment paper so that each malasada is on its own square. Working in batches, place the malasadas in the oil, paper side up, using

▶▶▶ Continued

tongs to peel off and discard the paper. Cook, flipping once, until puffed and golden, 2 to 3 minutes on each side. Transfer to a wire rack set on a baking sheet; let cool for 5 minutes, then toss with the sugar.

To make the pastry cream, in a saucepan, combine ¼ cup of the sugar and the milk and heat over medium heat for 2 to 3 minutes, until it begins to steam. Immediately remove the pan from the heat. Meanwhile, in a mixing bowl, whisk the remaining ½ cup sugar, egg yolks, cornstarch, and salt together until smooth. Slowly ladle about ¼ cup of the hot milk mixture into the egg yolks, whisking the entire time. Pour the tempered yolk mixture back into the saucepan and cook, whisking continuously, until thick, 3 to 4 minutes. Remove the saucepan from the heat and whisk in the butter, vanilla, and liliko'i juice; continue to whisk until smooth. Pour into a medium glass bowl and cover with plastic wrap directly touching the surface of the pastry cream. Set in a large bowl filled with ice water to cool.

Use a paring knife to cut a slit on one side into the middle of the malasadas. Fill a pastry bag fitted with a medium round tip halfway full with pastry cream. Pipe about 2 tablespoons of the filling into the slit in the malasadas. Refill the bag when it runs low.

Serve immediately, as malasadas are best fresh. Any leftovers can be stored in the refrigerator in a ziplock bag for up to 24 hours.

GAU

2 cups packed dark
brown sugar

½ teaspoon kosher salt

2¼ cups water

One 1-pound box mochiko
flour (see page 28)

3 tablespoons neutral oil

Makes one 8-inch round

ON THE MENU:

Shoyu 'Ahi Poke, page 38

Soy-Glazed Spam Musubi,
page 90

Boiled Peanuts, page 205

Gau is a rich, sweet, and sticky Chinese rice pudding that is a traditional Chinese New Year confection. Found in Chinese bakeries, Asian markets, and local grocery stores, gau's texture is similar to that of Japanese mochi. The trick to this treat is in the mixing, as you have to do it until no clumps remain! Gau is great with a cup of tea and can be eaten with your hands, as long as you aren't afraid to get a little sticky!

Fill a large pot with 2 inches of water. Fit the pot with a steamer basket and lid and bring the water to a simmer over medium heat. Line an 8-inch round cake pan with parchment paper, crinkling the paper to fit into the pan and up the sides. Place the round pan in the steamer basket and steam the paper for a minute or so to soften it. Remove from the steamer basket and gently press the paper into any remaining nooks and crannies that need to be filled.

In a saucepan, combine the brown sugar, salt, and 2¼ cups water and heat over medium-low heat for 2 to 3 minutes, until the mixture begins to simmer. Remove from the heat. In a bowl, beat the mochiko and the sugar mixture with a handheld electric mixer, on low speed, gradually increasing the speed to high. Mix until smooth, about 2 minutes, then add the oil and mix on medium speed until fully incorporated, about another minute. Pour the batter into the parchment-lined pan and rap the pan on the counter a few times to bring the air bubbles to the surface.

Carefully set the pan in the steamer basket and place a clean kitchen towel between the basket and the lid. This will help to prevent any condensation from dropping onto the gau's surface while it steams. Steam until the gau is cooked through and has completely set, 3 to 3½ hours, adding water to the pot if it runs low. Let cool completely before serving.

Slice the gau into wedges. The texture should be soft and gooey. It can be kept, covered in plastic wrap, at room temperature for up to 3 days. The gau will continue to firm up the longer it sits.

GUAVA
CAKE

Cake

2½ cups cake flour

2½ teaspoons baking powder

¾ teaspoon kosher salt

½ cup unsalted butter,
at room temperature

1¼ cups sugar

6 large egg whites

¼ cup neutral oil

1 cup whole milk

2 teaspoons vanilla extract

1 cup guava puree or
guava concentrate

3 squeezes of red gel coloring
(optional)

Frosting

1 cup heavy whipping cream

8 ounces cream cheese,
at room temperature

½ cup sugar

Pinch of kosher salt

2 squeezes of red gel food
coloring (optional)

½ cup guava puree or
guava concentrate

Makes 24 pieces

ON THE MENU:

Cone Sushi, page 51

Somen Salad, page 151

Teriyaki Beef Sticks, page 119

I like my desserts light as air and not too sweet, and this sheet cake fits the bill. It is great as a snack cake or served at a potluck. Made with guava puree, it's packed with flavor without being cloyingly sweet the way guava jams and jellies sometimes are. If you can't find fresh guava puree, you can use frozen guava concentrate. Just be sure that it's made with 100 percent juice and doesn't contain any extra sugar. If you can't find guava concentrate, you can make your own: boil 2 liters of 100 percent juice guava juice (Ceres is great) over high heat until it's reduced by more than half, about 40 minutes.

To make the cake, preheat the oven to 350°F. Line a 9 by 13-inch baking pan with parchment, leaving some overhang on the long sides.

In a bowl, combine the cake flour, baking powder, and kosher salt, whisking until combined. In a stand mixer fitted with the paddle attachment, combine the butter and sugar and beat on medium speed until well combined, about 3 minutes. Add the egg whites, in three additions, beating each addition until well combined, about 1 minute. Add the oil and mix until combined, about 1 minute more. In a separate bowl, whisk together the milk, vanilla, guava puree, and food coloring (if using). On low speed, alternate between adding the wet and dry ingredients, mixing each until combined before adding the next addition.

Pour the mixture into the parchment-lined pan and bake until a toothpick inserted into the center comes out clean, 25 to 30 minutes. Let the cake cool in the pan for 10 to 15 minutes before transferring it to a wire rack to cool completely.

To make the frosting, in a stand mixer fitted with the whisk attachment, whip the cream on medium speed for 1 to 2 minutes, until frothy. Gradually increase the speed to high and whip until it's light and fluffy with stiff peaks, another 2 to 3 minutes. Don't overwhip! Transfer the whipped cream to a bowl. Replace the bowl on the stand mixer and fit the machine with the paddle attachment; there's no need to clean the bowl. Place the cream cheese in the bowl and mix on medium speed for 2 to 3 minutes, until smooth. Add the sugar and kosher salt and increase the speed to high. Beat until light and fluffy, 2 to 3 minutes. Lower the speed to medium and add the food coloring, if desired. Gradually pour in the guava puree in four additions, making sure the puree is fully incorporated after every addition. Scrape down the sides with a rubber spatula after the second and the final addition. Increase the speed to high and beat until smooth and well incorporated, 1 to 2 minutes. Remove the bowl from the stand and, using the spatula, fold in the whipped cream in three additions, incorporating completely after each addition.

Spread the frosting on the cooled cake, using an offset spatula to smooth it over the edges, and chill for at least 2 hours before serving. Cut into twenty-four pieces and serve immediately.

SWEET BREAD ROLLS

Nowadays, sweet bread is closely associated with Hawai'i. While the most famous sweet bread might be King's Hawaiian, each island has its own local, favorite sweet bread spot. However, no matter what island you're on, all sweet bread originated from pão doce, or Portuguese sweet bread. Light, sweet, and so fluffy, this bread is great spread with butter and jam in the morning, served alongside Portuguese Bean Soup (page 97), or turned into mini Kālua Pig (page 83) sandwiches.

3¼ cups bread flour

3 tablespoons potato flour

1 teaspoon kosher salt

Two 0.25-ounce packages active dry yeast (4½ teaspoons total)

⅓ cup water, warmed (100° to 110°F), plus 1 teaspoon

¼ cup whole milk, warmed (100° to 110°F)

½ cup sugar

3 large eggs, 1 separated

1 teaspoon vanilla extract

6 tablespoons unsalted butter, at room temperature

Makes 12 rolls

ON THE MENU:

Kālua Pig, page 83

Side salad with Creamy Asian Dressing, page 217

Sweet Potato Haupia Bars, page 171

In a bowl, whisk 2¾ cups of the bread flour, the potato flour, and salt together and set aside.

Remove the bowl of your stand mixer and combine the remaining ½ cup bread flour with the active dry yeast and warm water, mixing it well with a wooden spoon. Mix until the mixture comes together and most of the dry bits are incorporated—it's okay if it looks a litte dry. Let the mixture rest for 45 minutes at room temperature, uncovered.

Return your stand mixer bowl to the mixer fitted with the paddle attachment. Turn the speed to low and add the milk, sugar, 2 eggs and 1 egg yolk, the vanilla, and butter—in that order—mixing until well combined, about 2 minutes. Turn off the mixer and change the attachment to the dough hook, scraping the paddle attachment clean. Turn the speed to low and add the dry ingredients, slowly increasing the speed to medium. Once combined, knead the dough on medium speed until the dough is smooth, about 5 minutes. Turn the dough out onto a clean surface and form into a ball. Clean the bowl and coat it lightly with neutral oil. Place the dough back in the bowl, turning once to coat both sides. Cover the bowl with a clean kitchen towel or plastic wrap and let rest in a warm spot until the dough has doubled in size, 1½ to 2 hours.

Lightly grease a 9 by 13-inch baking pan with neutral oil. Lightly punch down the dough and divide it into twelve equal pieces. Roll each piece into a ball and evenly space them in the pan. Cover the pan with the clean kitchen towel or lightly greased plastic wrap and let rise until doubled and puffy, 1 to 1½ hours.

Halfway through the rising time, preheat the oven to 350°F. In a small bowl, whisk the remaining egg white with the remaining 1 teaspoon water to make an egg-white wash. Brush the tops of the rolls with the egg-white wash, then bake until browned and cooked through, 20 to 25 minutes. If you have an instant-read thermometer, it should register 190°F when inserted into the middle of a roll. Let cool in the pan for 5 minutes before turning out onto a wire rack. Serve Warm. Leftover rolls can be stored in an airtight container at room temperature for 3 to 4 days.

SNACKS

('Ai Māmā)

Seemingly unrelated, these dishes all have one thing in common: they can be enjoyed on the go, while watching the nightly news, or beachside at sunset. Most of these foods can be paired perfectly with an ice-cold beverage, and all of them are great for snacking. Pickled Mango (page 194), Li Hing Gummy Bears (page 202), and Prune Mui (page 207) all have that sweet-sour-salty thing going on, while the rest of the snacks in this chapter will satisfy your salty-savory cravings.

PICKLED MANGO

1 cup water

¾ cup rice vinegar

¼ cup apple cider vinegar

⅔ cup sugar

1 tablespoon red li hing powder (see page 30)

1 teaspoon Hawaiian salt ('alaea)

2 large unripe, green mangoes

10 to 15 red li hing mui (see page 30)

Makes ½ gallon

ON THE MENU:

Boiled Peanuts, page 205

Pipi Kaula, page 199

Hurricane Popcorn, page 206

Every year, from late winter to early spring, the lush green mango trees are suddenly covered in blossoms. And that means just one thing: mango season is nearly here. Still, it feels like an eternity before those flowers transform into fruit, and it seems to take double that time for the fruit to ripen enough to perfume the air with its sweet aroma. That's where pickled mango comes in. Firm and unripe green mangoes are perfect for this dish, as long as they have firm, yellow flesh. Rapoza, Pirie, Haden, or any other variety of mango you can get your hands on will work. But don't use a ripe mango, as it won't yield that perfectly crunchy texture for the sweet-and-salty five-spice-laden pickle locals crave all year. Just ask anyone—even the thought of these mango slices makes the mouth water!

In a small nonreactive saucepan, combine the water with both vinegars, the sugar, red li hing powder, and salt and bring to a boil. When the sugar and salt have dissolved, remove the pan from the heat and let cool to room temperature.

Peel the mangoes using a vegetable peeler. If your mango is too soft to peel with the peeler, that means it's too soft to pickle; you need to use firm, unripe, green mangoes for this. Slice the mangoes into ¾-inch strips, carefully avoiding the seed in the middle and separating as much fruit from the seed as possible. Place the mango slices into a ½-gallon glass jar, layering in li hing mui as you go. Set aside.

Pour the cooled vinegar mixture over the mango slices and cover the jar with a lid. Store in the refrigerator for 3 days before serving. If stored in an airtight container, it will keep refrigerated for several weeks.

Note: You can omit the li hing mui and li hing powder if you'd like, but I'd recommend adding an extra tablespoon of sugar if you do.

MANAPUA

Bun (Bao)
¾ cup water, warmed
(100° to 110°F)

1¼ cups whole milk, warmed
(100° to 110°F)

Two 0.25-ounce packages
active dry yeast (4½ teaspoons
total)

1 teaspoon sugar, plus ¾ cup

4 cups all-purpose flour,
plus more as needed

2 cups cake flour

½ teaspoon kosher salt

⅓ cup neutral oil

Filling
1½ pounds Char Siu Pork
(page 86), minced

½ cup water

2 teaspoons cornstarch

2 teaspoons all-purpose flour

1 tablespoon sugar

¼ teaspoon kosher salt

Makes 12 manapua

ON THE MENU:

Chow Fun, page 148

Shoyu Chicken, page 103

Shave Ice, page 172

Manapua, Hawai'i's version of a Chinese char siu bao (steamed pork bun), is one of my favorite snacks. How it came to be known as the manapua is a story worth sharing. The name comes from the Hawaiian phrase "mea 'ono pua'a," which loosely translates to "delicious pork thing." How can you not love a delicious pork thing? Typically steamed, you can also find baked versions. My favorite manapua comes from Char Hung Sut on North Pauahi Street in Chinatown on the island of O'ahu. The giant manapua have the perfect bao (bun), both pillowy and chewy, and are very generously filled with the best char siu. This is my take on their classic.

To make the dough, combine the water, milk, yeast, and 1 teaspoon sugar in a bowl and whisk together. Let the mixture sit until the yeast is activated and foamy, about 10 minutes.

In the bowl of a stand mixer fitted with the dough hook, combine both flours, the salt, and the remaining ¾ cup sugar. Mix the dry ingredients together on low speed. Keep the mixer running and slowly pour in the yeast mixture followed by the oil. Increase the speed to medium and knead the dough until it is smooth and pulls away from the sides of the bowl, 5 to 7 minutes. If it does not start to pull away from the sides, add more flour, a tablespoon or two at a time. Turn the dough out onto a clean work surface quickly so that you can oil your stand mixer bowl. Transfer the dough back into the oiled bowl, flipping once to coat both sides, and cover the bowl loosely with plastic wrap or a clean kitchen towel. Let the dough rise until doubled in size, 1 to 2 hours.

While the dough is rising, cut twelve 4-inch squares of parchment paper for the bottom of the manapua.

To make the filling, put the char siu in a bowl. In a small saucepan, whisk together the water, cornstarch, all-purpose flour, sugar, and salt and bring to a boil over medium-high heat. Turn the heat to low and simmer for 1 minute, whisking continuously. Remove from the heat and pour over the char siu. Stir with a wooden spoon or toss with your hands to evenly coat the meat with the sauce.

Turn the dough out onto a clean work surface and divide it into twelve equal pieces. Transfer all but one piece back to the bowl, covering them with plastic wrap or a kitchen towel. Roll the piece of dough into a ball before flattening into a pancake with the palm of your hand. Use a rolling pin to roll the edges of the pancake out to a 5-inch round; you want the center of the dough to be a bit thicker—it should look like a little bump. This will help give the manapua a uniform thickness on the top and bottom. Add about ¼ cup filling to the center of the round, then bring the edges up and around the filling, pinching them together to seal in the filling. With the seam side down and your hand in a cupping

▶▶▶ Continued

motion, gently roll the manapua into a ball with a few circular motions. Place the round ball, seam side down, on one of the precut parchment squares. Cover the ball with a clean kitchen towel and repeat until all the dough has been used. Let the dough rise for 30 minutes.

Meanwhile, bring a large pot of water to boil with the lid on. Set a steamer basket over it and turn the heat to low, keeping the water at a simmer. Place the manapua with the parchment squares in the basket, spacing them about an inch apart. If you are using a metal steamer or a glass lid, place a clean kitchen towel between the basket and the lid to capture the condensation. Steam until the buns are light and fluffy, 15 to 20 minutes; they should be touching or almost touching. Transfer to a wire rack, cover with a clean towel, and let cool for 5 to 10 minutes before serving.

Store leftovers in a ziplock bag in the refrigerator or freezer. To reheat, simply wrap in a damp paper towel and microwave for 30 seconds or resteam them in a steamer basket for 10 minutes, until heated through.

PIPI KAULA

½ cup soy sauce (shoyu)

2 tablespoons rice vinegar

1 teaspoon sesame oil

1 teaspoon Hawaiian salt ('alaea)

3 tablespoons sugar

1 teaspoon freshly ground black pepper

1 garlic clove, peeled and finely minced or grated

1 Hawaiian chili pepper (nīoi), crushed

1½ pounds flank steak, cut into 2-inch-wide strips

Neutral oil, for frying

Serves 4 to 6

ON THE MENU:

Boiled Peanuts, page 205
Pickled Mango, page 194
Shoyu 'Ahi Poke, page 38

Hawai'i's history of ranching dates back to the 1830s, when Mexican cowboys came to help manage the islands' wild cattle problem. The Hawaiians took quickly to the culture of ranching, and so emerged the Hawaiian paniolo (cowboy). Pipi kaula is a dish that came from this ranching culture. Back in the day, salted beef strips were dried in the sun, while today, thanks to modern technology, they can be made indoors. Think of it as Hawaiian beef jerky, with a bit of local flavor in the form of soy sauce (shoyu), sesame oil, and sugar.

In a bowl, whisk the soy sauce, rice vinegar, sesame oil, salt, sugar, black pepper, garlic, and chili pepper to form a marinade. Place the meat in a gallon-size ziplock bag or a baking dish and pour the marinade over. Seal the bag or cover the dish and refrigerate for at least 8 hours, preferably overnight.

Preheat the oven to 175°F. Set a wire rack on a rimmed baking sheet lined with aluminum foil and set the strips of meat on the rack. Bake until the meat has a chewy texture, similar to a jerky, about 5 hours. Store in an airtight container in the refrigerator for up to 1 week.

Set a skillet over medium heat and add a teaspoon of neutral oil. Fry until the meat is heated through, 2 to 3 minutes on each side. Cut into small pieces and serve warm.

BAKED TARO AND SWEET POTATO CHIPS

Nutty, sweet, and salty, the combination of taro and sweet potato is almost addictive. Baked instead of fried, these chips are the perfect paring with a pau hana (work is over) mai tai or beer. And you'll be amazed by how quick and easy they are to pull together! Eat them as a snack with some Pickled Mango (page 194) or Prune Mui (page 207), or use them as a vehicle for Shoyu 'Ahi Poke (page 38)—think fancy appetizer. No matter how you choose to serve them, you won't be disappointed.

Preheat the oven to 350°F. Using a mandoline or sharp knife, thinly slice the taro root and sweet potatoes into thin rounds—as thin as possible. Evenly drizzle two large rimmed baking sheets with olive oil and arrange the rounds on the sheets, the taro on one sheet and the sweet potato on the other, in a single layer. Season with salt and pepper, then evenly drizzle olive oil over the rounds. Bake for 20 minutes, until crisp and golden, flipping the slices halfway through the baking time. Serve warm or let cool to room temperature. The chips will keep in an airtight container at room temperature for up to 2 days.

1 large taro (kalo) root (2 to 3 pounds), cleaned and peeled

2 large Okinawan sweet potatoes (1½ pounds), cleaned and peeled

Olive oil, for drizzling

Kosher salt and freshly ground black pepper

Serves 4 to 6

ON THE MENU:

Lumpia (page 48)
Cone Sushi (page 51)
Save Ice (page 172)

LI HING GUMMY BEARS

1 pound gummy bears

½ cup warm water (85°F)

1 tablespoon red li hing powder (see page 30)

Makes 1 pound

ON THE MENU:

Boiled Peanuts, page 205

Prune Mui, page 207

Hurricane Popcorn, page 206

If you've ever had sticky li hing gummy bears, you'll know that it's a snack that's hard to quit. What you might not realize is how easy it is to make your own. The secret? Li hing sauce is actually made with just a little warm water. So simple—try it for yourself!

Place the gummy bears in a colander and pour the warm water over them. Gently toss to evenly disperse the water. The gummy bears should make their own "sauce." Immediately sprinkle the li hing powder onto the bears and transfer to an airtight container to store up to 6 months.

Note: Li hing powder is also great sprinkled on fresh fruits, like sliced pineapple, orange wedges, and sliced mango!

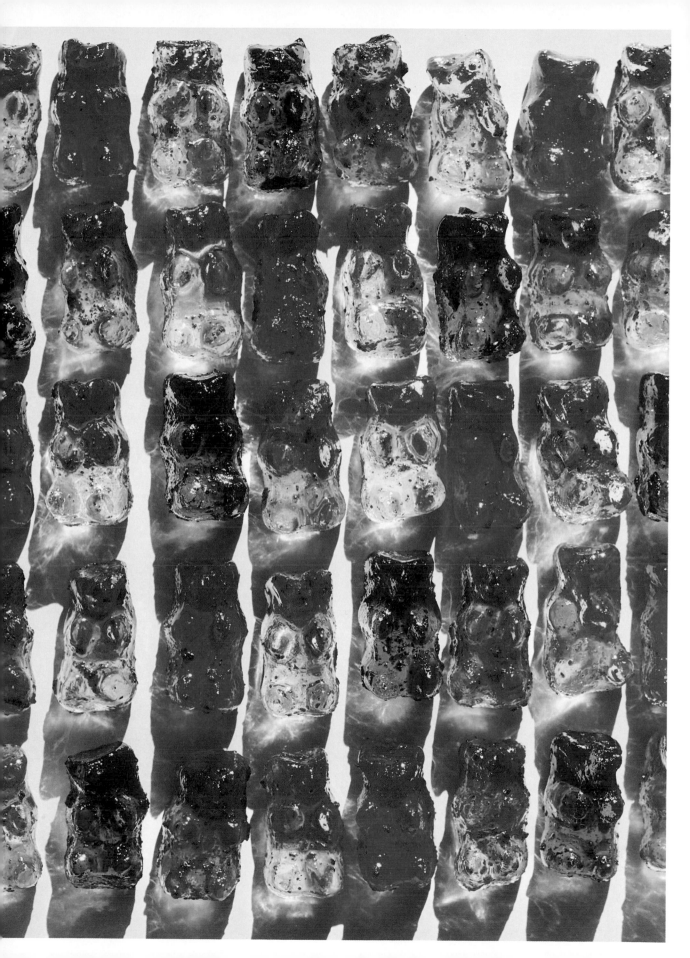

BOILED PEANUTS

2 pounds raw shell-on peanuts

4 quarts water

⅓ cup Hawaiian salt ('alaea)

2 whole star anise

Makes 2 pounds

ON THE MENU:

Pickled Mango, page 194

Hurricane Popcorn, page 206

Baked Taro and Sweet Potato Chips, page 201

Usually found alongside poke counters, boiled peanuts are the ultimate pau hana (work is over) snack. My mom says they were made for beer. Back in the day, they were sold in brown paper bags, but now they're usually packaged in plastic bags. To make your own, look for raw shell-on peanuts at an Asian market or order them on Amazon.

Place the peanuts in a colander and rinse well; you may need to do this in two batches. Meanwhile, combine the water, salt, and star anise in a large pot and give the pot a quick swirl to combine everything. Add the rinsed peanuts to the pot and place a large bowl filled with water (if necessary) over the peanuts to weigh them down. Soak the peanuts in the salt solution at room temperature for 24 hours.

Remove the bowl and bring the pot to a boil over high heat. Once it is boiling, turn the heat to medium-low and cover the pot with a lid. Simmer for up to 2 hours; you can start checking the doneness of your peanuts after an hour. To do so, simply remove a peanut from the water and let it cool slightly before shelling and eating. If it's tender with a little crunch, it's done.

When the peanuts are cooked, remove the pot from the heat and take off the lid. Let the peanuts cool in the solution for 1 hour before draining them into a colander. Serve the peanuts warm or let cool to room temperature, then transfer to a ziplock plastic bag and chill in the refrigerator. They will keep refrigerated for up to 5 days.

HURRICANE POPCORN

6 tablespoons salted butter

8 to 9 cups freshly popped popcorn (about ⅓ cup unpopped kernels)

¼ cup nori komi furikake (see page 31)

1 cup mochi crunch or Japanese rice crackers (arare)

Serves 2 to 4

ON THE MENU:

Pickled Mango, page 194

Prune Mui, page 207

Baked Taro and Sweet Potato Chips, page 201

The one thing I really miss about Hawaiian movie theaters is the ability to eat arare (mochi crunch or Japanese rice crackers) in the auditorium. The distinct smell and loud crunch of the crackers is hard to disguise, and while I've tried once or twice in LA to sneak them in, my seatmates are always quick to turn and stare. Hurricane popcorn is both arare and popcorn, boosted with furikake and lots of butter. When purchasing arare, look for Tomoe brand, the one in the yellow bag. The secret to this popcorn is the browned butter; without it, you're left with soggy popcorn!

Melt the butter in a small saucepan over medium-high heat. Cook the butter until it becomes foamy, then turn the heat to medium-low and let it simmer and bubble for 2 to 3 minutes, until the bubbling stops. At this point, you should see lightly browned bits on the bottom of the pan. Drizzle the butter, being careful to avoid pouring out the browned bits, over the popped popcorn. Sprinkle with the furikake and toss with the arare. Hurricane Popcorn is best eaten the same day.

PRUNE MUI

2 pounds dark brown sugar

1½ cups fresh lemon juice (about 8 lemons)

3 tablespoons whiskey

1½ teaspoons Chinese five-spice powder

2 tablespoons red li hing powder (see page 30)

3 tablespoons Hawaiian salt ('alaea)

½ teaspoon whole cloves

3 ounces red li hing mui (see page 30)

5 pounds dried fruit of your choice (such as pitted prunes, dried apricots, dried tart cherries, dried cranberries)

Makes 1 gallon

ON THE MENU:

Hurricane Popcorn, facing page

Boiled Peanuts, page 205

Li Hing Gummy Bears, page 202

Sweet and sour, and definitely a bit sticky, prune mui is a unique treat. Made with preserved fruits, li hing powder, and a combination of spices, lemon juice, and sugar, this snack is one of my personal favorites. This recipe yields a large batch, making it ideal for preparing during the holiday season to give as gifts. It takes about a week for the mixture to be ready to consume, so plan ahead.

In a large pot, combine the brown sugar, lemon juice, whiskey, five-spice powder, li hing powder, salt, and whole cloves, mixing with a wooden spoon to combine. Heat over medium-low heat until the sugar dissolves. Remove from the heat and let cool for 10 minutes. Add the li hing mui and the dried fruit and mix well with a wooden spoon to evenly coat the fruit. Transfer to two ½-gallon jars (or multiple smaller jars), packing the fruit tightly. Disperse the extra syrup evenly among the jars and let cool completely before covering the jars tightly with their lids.

Let the fruit sit in the jars in a cool, dry, dark place for 1 week, shaking and rotating the jars daily. The fruit will be soft and sticky when it's ready to serve. Serve a small amount in a bowl and use your fingers or chopsticks to eat it. Store in an airtight container in the refrigerator for up to 1 month.

DRINKS

(Pau Hana)

Pau hana (work is over) is an important part of the day for locals. It's the time after work or school when family and friends take a break so they can unwind, relax, and enjoy the moment together. While most of the drinks in this chapter are nonalcoholic, feel free to add your favorite spirit to liven them up, or check out the Mai Tai (page 213).

POG

1½ cups guava juice,
or ¾ cup guava puree
plus ¾ cup water

1½ cups liliko'i (passion
fruit) juice

1 cup fresh orange juice

¼ cup fresh lime juice
(optional)

¼ cup 1:1 Simple Syrup
(facing page)

Ice, for serving

Orange slices, for garnish

Serves 4

Passion orange guava (POG) juice is a drink that locals are very fond of. It's ubiquitous, so much so that I never thought of it as just a Hawai'i thing. I grew up drinking Meadow Gold POG, the one in the bright orange carton, at home, and cans of Hawaiian Sun's Pass-o-Guava after soccer games, at potlucks, or at the beach. You can imagine my surprise freshman year of college in San Diego when there was no POG to be found. I recently tried POG for the first time in years and was blown away by how sweet it is. This is my take on a slightly less sweet, but still very POG-y, POG. The optional lime juice adds a bright tartness that really jazzes everything up.

Combine the guava juice, liliko'i juice, orange juice, lime juice (if using), and simple syrup in a large glass measuring cup or bowl. Whisk together and serve over ice. Garnish each glass with an orange slice.

PLANTATION ICED TEA

3 cups freshly brewed green
tea, at room temperature

⅓ cup fresh pineapple juice

¼ cup Ginger Simple Syrup
(facing page)

¼ cup fresh lime juice

Ice, for serving

Fresh mint sprigs, for garnish

Pineapple wedges, for garnish

Serves 4

Similar to a sweet tea or an Arnold Palmer, plantation iced tea is essentially a blend of iced tea and, most commonly, pineapple juice. While typically made with black tea and sweetened with simple syrup, green tea and ginger simple syrup brighten up this plantation era–inspired classic.

Combine the green tea, pineapple juice, simple syrup, and lime juice in a large glass measuring cup or bowl and whisk together. Cover the cup or bowl with plastic wrap and refrigerate until cold, about 1 hour. Serve over ice and garnish each glass with mint and a pineapple wedge.

FRUIT PUNCH

1 cup guava juice, or ½ cup fresh guava puree plus ½ cup water

1 cup fresh pineapple Juice

1 cup fresh orange juice

1 cup liliko'i (passion fruit) juice

¼ cup fresh lime juice

½ cup strawberry juice

½ cup 1:1 Simple Syrup (below)

Orange slices, for garnish

Serves 4 to 6

Growing up, I was like every kid of the 1990s. When the Hawaiian Punch commercial came on TV, I was sold. Never mind our access to fresh fruit juices—no, no, I needed Hawaiian Punch. And while I pleaded and begged for it, I am glad to have also found this fruit punch. Made with (mostly) fresh juices, this is a Hawaiian punch I can get behind.

Combine the guava juice, pineapple juice, orange juice, liliko'i juice, lime juice, strawberry juice, and simple syrup in a large glass measuring cup or bowl. Whisk together and serve over ice. Garnish each glass with an orange slice.

1:1 SIMPLE SYRUP

Makes 1 cup

This is something I always keep on hand. It's great for everything from iced tea to cocktails. Called "simple" for a reason, it's made with equal parts of sugar and water. What makes it so great is that it evenly sweetens your drinks without any grittiness from the sugar.

1 cup sugar

1 cup water

In a saucepan, combine the sugar and water. Bring to a boil over medium-high heat, stirring with a wooden spoon to dissolve the sugar. The liquid should go from cloudy to clear. Remove from the heat and let cool completely before using. Store the syrup in an airtight container in the refrigerator for up to 1 month.

GINGER SIMPLE SYRUP

Makes 1 cup

A variation on classic 1:1 Simple Syrup, this is my go-to for adding a little extra kick to my drinks.

1 cup granulated sugar

1 cup filtered water

One 1-inch piece fresh ginger, peeled and thinly sliced

In a saucepan, combine the sugar, water, and ginger. Bring to a boil over medium-high heat, stirring with a wooden spoon to dissolve the sugar. The liquid should go from cloudy to clear. Remove from the heat and let steep for about 1 hour before removing the ginger. Store the syrup in an airtight container in the refrigerator for up to 1 week.

HONEY SYRUP

Makes 2 cups

Like 1:1 Simple Syrup, honey syrup calls for equal parts of honey and water. It's a great way to impart the complex flavors of honey—floral, nutty, and even earthy notes— into your drinks or cocktails without worrying about clumpy bits of honey floating around!

1 cup honey

1 cup boiling hot water

In a bowl, whisk the honey and boiling water together until combined. Let cool completely before transferring the syrup to an airtight container. Store in the refrigerator for up to 1 month.

MAI TAI

Ice

2 ounces dark molasses rum (like El Dorado 8-Year Demerara Rum)

1 ounce light pure cane rum (like Batiste Rhum Ecoiste)

½ ounce Honey Syrup (page 211)

½ ounce orgeat syrup (Small Hand Foods and Liquid Alchemist are great options)

¾ ounce fresh lime juice

Spritz of Angostura bitters (use an atomizer or spray bottle)

Lime wheel, for garnish

Serves 1

An iconic tiki beverage, the mai tai is commonly associated with Hawai'i, despite its California origin. Whether you believe Don the Beachcomber or Trader Vic invented the drink, its strong tie to the islands remains. If you've ordered them in the past, chances are you've had varied experiences, ranging from great to terrible and everything in between.

Rather than leave it to chance, I enlisted the help of one of Hawai'i's most decorated bartenders, two-time "World's Best Mai Tai" champion, 2014 "Shake It Up!" Cocktail Competition winner, and US representative for the IBA World Cocktail Competition Justin Park of Bar Leather Apron in Honolulu, O'ahu. This is his take on a classic mai tai, where he forgoes the traditional floating of the rums to create a well-balanced cocktail that's great from start to finish.

Fill a double old-fashioned glass with ice and set it aside to chill. In a cocktail shaker with ice, combine both rums, the honey syrup, orgeat syrup, and lime juice. Shake. Strain into the ice-filled glass. Evenly spritz the top of the drink with bitters and garnish with a lime wheel before severing.

BARTENDER'S NOTE

When it comes to mai tai, or any cocktail for that matter, the number-one thing to focus on is balance. What I enjoy about a mai tai is the ability to taste all the ingredients individually, while the overall flavor in the finish of the cocktail is very harmonious. For example, the rum is present, but only enough to give you a taste. Then comes the back and forth of citrus and sweet, but the finish is everything at once. I am not sure if this is making sense, but it is how I go about creating a cocktail.

When you look at what is known as the 1944 original mai tai from Trader Vic's, you see this recipe:

1 ounce lime juice, ½ ounce orange Curaçao, ¼ ounce orgeat syrup, ¼ ounce 1:1 Simple Syrup, 1 ounce aged Jamaican rum, 1 ounce aged Martinique agricole rhum

The short story is the cocktail contains two parts spirit, one part sweet, and one part citrus. I know this may be getting boring, but it's an easy way to understand how to start when making a mai tai at home. Take the three elements and replace a sweet for a sweet, or a different citrus for a citrus. Try different types of rum.

—Justin Park

SAUCES

I consider these recipes to be proverbial workhorses in that they all function in more than one way. You can finish a salad with Creamy Asian Dressing (page 217), but you can also drizzle it over your Mochiko Chicken (page 100) or dip your Chicken Katsu (page 111) into it. The Dynamite Sauce (page 217) is great with everything from Spam Fried Rice (page 89) to Maui-Style Kalbi Short Ribs (page 120). Get creative with these sauces; they're made to do double duty.

DYNAMITE SAUCE

½ cup Best Foods (or Hellmann's) mayonnaise

1 tablespoon rice vinegar

1½ teaspoons sugar

1½ teaspoons sriracha

1 tablespoon smelt roe (masago)

Makes about ½ cup

Drizzle this on everything from Mochiko Chicken (page 100) to Beef Chili (page 128)—don't knock it 'til you try it! This Japanese sauce was made for just about everything.

In a small bowl, whisk together the mayonnaise, rice vinegar, sugar, and sriracha. Gently mix in the smelt roe. Transfer to a jar with a lid and store in the refrigerator for up to 3 days.

CREAMY ASIAN DRESSING

½ cup Best Foods (or Hellmann's) mayonnaise

1 tablespoon soy sauce (shoyu)

2 tablespoons rice vinegar

⅛ teaspoon sesame oil

3 tablespoons sugar

1 tablespoon toasted sesame seeds

Makes 1 cup

My friend Kammy and her husband have a mochiko chicken cone business. I dream about the secret creamy dressing they drizzle on their mochiko chicken. This dressing tastes close to theirs and is great for drizzling, dipping, or dressing a salad.

In a bowl, whisk together the mayonnaise, soy sauce, rice vinegar, sesame oil, sugar, and sesame seeds until the consistency is thick like honey. Transfer to a jar with a lid and refrigerate for 2 hours. Let the dressing sit at room temperature for about 15 minutes before using. Store in the refrigerator for up to 1 week.

PAPAYA SEED DRESSING

Flesh and seeds from 1 ripe Solo papaya (see page 34)

2 tablespoons fresh lime juice

½ teaspoon Dijon mustard

1 shallot, peeled and finely chopped

¼ teaspoon kosher salt

¼ teaspoon freshly ground black pepper

1 tablespoon sugar

¼ cup neutral oil

Makes about ½ cup

This is a multipurpose dressing and sauce, and what I love about this one is its complexity: it has a buttery sweetness, thanks to the papaya, but with the kick of mustard and lime and a touch of texture from the addition of the seeds. It can be used much like Dynamite Sauce (page 217) and Creamy Asian Dressing (page 217), on everything from salads to chicken.

In a blender, combine the flesh and seeds of the papaya with the lime juice, Dijon mustard, shallot, salt, pepper, sugar, and oil and process on high speed for 1½ to 2 minutes, until smooth. Use right away, or transfer to an airtight jar or bottle and store in the refrigerator for up to 1 week.

LILIKO'I VINAIGRETTE

¼ cup liliko'i (passion fruit) pulp (see page 159)

2 tablespoons rice vinegar

2 teaspoons Dijon mustard

1 tablespoon sugar

¼ cup neutral oil or olive oil

¼ teaspoon kosher salt

¼ teaspoon freshly ground black pepper

Makes about ½ cup

Sweet, tart, and fragrant, this vinaigrette livens up even the dullest of salads.

In a blender, combine the liliko'i pulp with the rice vinegar, mustard, sugar, oil, salt, and pepper and process on high speed for 2 to 3 minutes, until smooth. Use right away, or transfer to an airtight jar or bottle and store in the refrigerator for up to 1 week.

GUAVA DRESSING

¼ cup guava juice

2 tablespoons red wine vinegar

1 tablespoon minced Maui onion

1 teaspoon Dijon mustard

¼ cup neutral oil or olive oil

¼ teaspoon kosher salt

¼ teaspoon freshly ground black pepper

Makes about ½ cup

Quick, easy to make, but most of all delicious, this dressing is great on salads but also doubles as a marinade for chicken!

In a blender, combine the guava juice with the vinegar, onion, mustard, oil, salt, and pepper and process on high speed for 1 to 2 minutes, until smooth. Use right away, or transfer to an airtight jar or bottle and store in the refrigerator for up to 1 week.

CHILI PEPPER WATER

1 cup water

¼ cup rice vinegar

1 teaspoon Hawaiian salt ('alaea)

1 garlic clove, peeled and smashed

4 Hawaiian chili peppers (nīoi), 2 finely chopped and 2 left whole

Makes 10 ounces

You can't walk into a local restaurant without the familiar sight of chili pepper water. It's usually in a repurposed ketchup bottle, or something similar, and is the local answer to Tabasco.

In a small saucepan over medium-high heat, combine the water with the vinegar, salt, garlic, and chili peppers and bring to a boil. Remove from the heat and let cool completely before transferring it to an airtight jar. Let sit in the refrigerator for 2 days before using so that the flavors meld. Store in the refrigerator for up to 1 month.

MAHALO

To each and every person who helped make this book possible, let me start with mahalo, or thank you. And then add about one hundred more thank-yous to that. Without each and every one of you, this book would not have happened.

Ten Speed Press, you guys are my dream come true. I'm so grateful to all of you for rallying behind this book from the start and for shepherding it out into the world. Kelly Snowden, I feel lucky to have an editor like you for a book like this. Thank you for all your guidance, your patience, your wit, and for believing in this book as much as I do. This book is as much mine as it is yours, and I hope you love the end result as much as I do. And mahalo for all the laughs along the way. Emma Campion and Annie Marino, thank you for your magnanimous flexibility, your trained eyes, and your trust. Ashley Pierce, you were a joy to work with and I appreciated each and every note you sprinkled into the edits and queries! To Windy Dorresteyn, Alison Renzulli, Kristin Casemore, Jane Chinn, Kathy Brock, and Sharon Silva, mahalo, mahalo, mahalo.

Joan Kysar, I couldn't have written even a page of this book without you. Thank you for being my #1 recipe tester; I know that it was not a responsibility you took lightly, and your notes were invaluable. Each recipe is better because you made it better. Also, your mochiko chicken will forever be better than mine, no matter how many times I make it, so please know that I will never stop asking for it.

Mitch Kysar, you taught me how to appreciate all aspects of food. You helped me build a somewhat discerning palate while showing me how beautiful food can be. While I may have led you to believe the opposite, especially during my teen years, I'm grateful for everything you've taught me. Thank you for lending a sympathetic ear during this book-writing process, reading all my rough drafts, and for always supplying the wine-down.

Moses Aipa, I know it's been a struggle watching me tear the kitchen, dining room, living room, and office apart while creating this book. I appreciate your patience, and I thank you for all those times you washed the dishes when I was too tired to even look at them. Thank you for your guidance, for your art direction, and your creativity. You are the best hand model! Thank you for coming to Hawai'i every time I needed to research or shoot something for this book. And thank you for designing this beautiful book with Emma and Annie.

Vienna Sausage, thank you for forcing me to get outside every three to four hours. For demanding sun breaks. For the countless snuggles, for licking away my tears of frustration after the fifth round of sweet-bread testing, for always being around, and for listening to my terrible singing day in and out. You are the best dog a girl could ask for.

To the Aipa and Ishimaru ohana: Hilary, Nathan, Lena, Isaiah, Harvey, Mari, Daniel, Jonah, Kristie, Bert, and Shelbie. Mahalo for all the love and support throughout this process. Mahalo for being so generous with your knowledge, time, and for teaching me how special an imu really is. Mahalo for putting together the most magical lū'au imaginable and for somehow making that gorgeous sunset appear. And mahalo for sharing your Moses with me.

To my super-hero of an agent, Nicole Tourtelot, you are the real deal. I can't imagine any part of this journey without you. You made every step as easy as possible and did it with so much style and grace.

Brooklyn Dombroski, hi. You are insanely talented and I am so lucky to call you my friend. Thank you for all the beautiful moments you captured. I love looking at Hawai'i through your lens. Thank you for agreeing to work on this book with me.

Justin Park, you are one of the most gracious and kindhearted people out there—not to mention, one of the most talented. Thank you for being my boss way back when and for contributing such a pivotal recipe to this book. Cheers to many more years of friendship!

Jordan Higa, thank you for working your magic and bringing the produce and map to life! That extra bit of illo POP pulled everything together and I'm so grateful you came on board!

Onaona Thoene, it seems like you have seen me through it all and have made me better every step of the way. Thank you for taking the time to make this book the best it can be.

Lily Diamond, I couldn't have done this without you. Thank you for being my biggest cheerleader, for guiding me through the book process, from start to finish, and for always believing in this book and well, me!

To everyone who came for 'ohana dinners, you guys are forever ohana now! Mahalo to the Ruffing 'ohana, the Musser 'ohana, Dane Story, the Christensen 'ohana, Valerie Shagday, Jesson Duller, Christina Laguens, Chase Wayton, Morgan Suzuki, Tiffany Tse, Eric Ideta, the Meinel 'ohana, Mikey Jergentz, Nicole Tourtelot, and Tremaine Tucker for hanging out, trying the goods, the not quite there yet, and for keeping me company.

To the Kido 'ohana, I couldn't have dreamed up a more perfect location and day for our lū'au. Thank you. And to Onaona Thoene, Brooklyn Dombroski, Kaiwi Berry, Johnson Young, the Kysar 'ohana, the Pascher 'ohana, the Rose + Fisher 'ohana, Kaimana Plemer, Kim Shibata, Jade Snow (you were there in spirit), the Kaneshiro 'ohana, the Ishimaru 'ohana, and, of course, the Aipa 'ohana, thank you for making the trek out to the North Shore and for sharing that special January day with us. To the Snow 'ohana for opening up your home to us, mahalo.

To my SLAMM tribe—Lily Diamond, Molly Yeh, Michelle Lopez, and Stephanie Le—you got me through so many unknowns (I'm sorry for asking soooo many questions), built me up, and kept me sane. You guys are my rocks, my heroes, and an endless source of inspiration. Love you ladies to pieces.

To my LA ohana—Jackie, Bob, Wyatt, Mason, Diera, and Jared—mahalo for the love you've shown us over the years and a special thank-you for the extra love you've given this book.

To my generous recipe testers—Joan Kysar, Molly Yeh, Michelle Lopez, Sara Tan Christensen, Diera Story, Lily Diamond, Jackie Ruffing, Jennifer Yee, and Natasha Feldman—mahalo for your invaluable input and for putting in all that time!

To all the wonderful brands that I worked with to build this book, your pieces are loved, your product is valued, and I am a huge fan of all of you. Mahalo to Meredith Bradford of the Zwilling Group, Julia Lemke of Earthen, Shawn Kam of Luvhaus, Karina Subijana of Altar Ceramics, Justin Caraco Ceramics, Tina Huang of Ren•Vois, Margaux Gonyea at Williams Sonoma, Nate Volk and Brandon at Pacific Helicopter Tours, Lindsey Ozawa at Kāko'o 'Ōiwi, and Melissa's Produce.

To the incredible community of bloggers who have encouraged, guided, and totally inspired me throughout the years—Gaby Dalkin, Shelly Westerhausen, Kristan Raines, Lyndsay Sung, Adrianna Adarme, Billy Green, Sarah Menanix, Alanna Taylor-Tobin, Betty Liu, Erin Clarkson, Haley Hunt Davis, Emily Stoffel, Lindsey Love, Courtney Chun, Sherrie Castellano, Cynthia Chen McTernan, Cindy Ensley, Teri Fischer, Jenny Park, Jodi Moreno, Jessica Merchant, Sarah Kieffer, Ashlae Warner, Jonathan Melendez, Nik Sharma, Kathryn Taylor, Erin Alderson, Melissa Coleman, Gerry Spiers, Brooke Bass, Hetty McKinnon, Erika Raxworthy, and Brandon Matzek—thank you for being so BA!

Finally, to all the readers of *Fix Feast Flair*, mahalo for coming along on this journey with me. It's bigger and better than I could have ever dreamed, and it's because of all of you.

INDEX

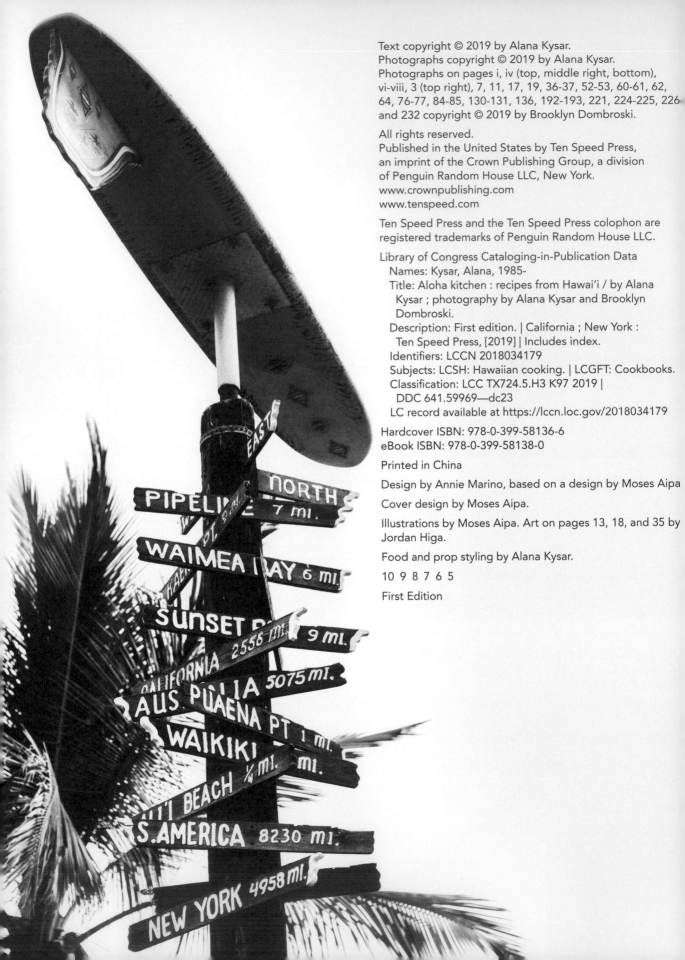

Published in the United States by Ten Speed Press,
an imprint of the Crown Publishing Group, a division
of Penguin Random House LLC, New York.
www.crownpublishing.com
www.tenspeed.com

Ten Speed Press and the Ten Speed Press colophon are
registered trademarks of Penguin Random House LLC.

Library of Congress Cataloging-in-Publication Data
  Names: Kysar, Alana, 1985-
  Title: Aloha kitchen : recipes from Hawai'i / by Alana
    Kysar ; photography by Alana Kysar and Brooklyn
    Dombroski.
  Description: First edition. | California ; New York :
    Ten Speed Press, [2019] | Includes index.
  Identifiers: LCCN 2018034179
  Subjects: LCSH: Hawaiian cooking. | LCGFT: Cookbooks.
  Classification: LCC TX724.5.H3 K97 2019 |
    DDC 641.59969—dc23
  LC record available at https://lccn.loc.gov/2018034179

Hardcover ISBN: 978-0-399-58136-6
eBook ISBN: 978-0-399-58138-0

Printed in China

Design by Annie Marino, based on a design by Moses Aipa

Cover design by Moses Aipa.

Illustrations by Moses Aipa. Art on pages 13, 18, and 35 by
Jordan Higa.

Food and prop styling by Alana Kysar.

10 9 8 7 6 5

First Edition